Joe's

expert gardening guide

create your own
modern
space

Collins

Published by Collins
An imprint of HarperCollins Publishers
Westerhill Road, Bishopbriggs, Glasgow G64 2QT
www.harpercollins.co.uk
collins.reference@harpercollins.co.uk

HarperCollins Publishers
1st Floor, Watermarque Building, Ringsend Road,
Dublin 4, Ireland

© HarperCollins Publishers 2022
Text © Joe Swift
Cover image © Joe Swift / Mabo / Alamy Stock
Photo

A catalogue record for this book is available from
the British Library

ISBN 978-0-00-846112-6

10 9 8 7 6 5 4 3 2 1

Printed in Slovenia by GPS Group

Thanks to my agents, Charlotte Robertson and
Debbie Scheisse, and everyone at HarperCollins
Publishers including Gerry Breslin, Gordon
MacGilp, Lauren Murray and Kevin Robbins.

Photo credits

Joe's

expert gardening guide

create your own
modern
space

introduction

design considerations

hard landscaping

Introduction

Modern gardens are for modern living. They are well-designed plots that both look great and function well.

Some may interpret 'modern' as 'minimal'. Yes, they can be minimal, pared back to the basic elements, perhaps with a higher proportion of hard landscaping to soft in some cases, but that preconception is never a given. There are many great modern spaces made up of predominantly 'soft elements' of lawns, plants and wildflowers; as with all good garden design and gardening, it's how they're conceived, put together and developed over time that makes the difference. Modern spaces certainly don't have to be in an urban setting either or alongside a modern property and can look stunning in any locale whether it's rural, suburban or right in the heart of a city.

With a clear vision, the results can be spectacular. Many garden styles mimic nature to a degree whereas modern gardens are more likely to take their inspiration from it and then distil, stylise and often simplify it. 'Clean lines' are a signature of a modern space. Sure, straight lines and rectilinear grid layouts can work well in the right setting, often leading to a garden with an organised, modern feel but there are many fabulous contemporary gardens based on sinuous, fluid lines and smooth arcs too.

I believe gardening should never feel like a chore. The amount of time one has to garden is a huge factor these days so perhaps a modern space is the perfect solution for you? The combined layout, choice of landscaping materials, plants and planting style can make a significant difference to the amount of time you'll need to put into it. There are also many time-saving products like computer-operated irrigation systems and robot mowers that can be adopted to potentially allow you to spend more time on the most pleasurable aspects of gardening, or simply more time to chill and entertain in it.

You may know you want a modern garden but have inherited a plot with many disparate elements? Before ripping them all out and starting over with a blank canvas, it's important to consider the value of each. I've designed and viewed many modern gardens that have kept their 'sense of place' by retaining some valuable older features and characterful plants, yet have cleverly edited and updated them to fit with the new vision. Landscaping materials, plants and planting style can make a significant difference to the amount of time you'll need to put into it.

I view versatility as a key component of a contemporary space too. Perhaps an outdoor room that performs well for a variety of uses (relaxing/dining/entertaining/exercise/gardening), yet isn't dominated by any one of them and always feels like a sanctuary to escape into and connect with nature.

I have been designing and landscaping contemporary spaces for over 30 years. This book captures my thought process and approach. A great garden can take years to develop and is never truly finished, yet I can't stress how important it is to have a clear idea of where you're heading first, which will save you time, money and heartache in the long run. I hope this book provides both inspiration and practical advice to give you the confidence to create something special, unique and personal in your outside space.

design
considerations

assessing your plot

Designing a successful garden goes way beyond just putting in materials and plants and standing back to admire it, as if it's a static installation that will stay the same forever. The fifth dimension of 'time' plays a huge part and is something to be respected and celebrated as it keeps our gardens fresh, changing throughout the seasons and developing year on year.

Longevity is the key to creating a really successful garden and to do this you'll need to understand as much about your unique site as possible as it will affect how you lay it out as well as what plants will thrive where. An experienced gardener will understand the range of possibilities and restrictions from the soil and aspect and work within them; a 'virgin' gardener will need to learn and along the way will experience both success and failure on occasion (as we all have and still do!).

Analysing the site specifics and being scientific (the art is there but comes later) will get the best from it and see quicker results. I can't stress enough how important it is to 'go with' the existing natural elements of your garden's aspect, soil and setting to achieve success, rather than fighting what you have.

sketch out a site analysis

Here we're 'building up a profile' of your garden to help make sense of it: the good, bad and ugly! Roughly measure out (or approach it more accurately if you want to develop a garden plan yourself in future) your garden. As you go through the process below, sketch onto it a few bubbles and arrows and annotate key and notable issues like 'full shade', 'steep slope', 'privacy issue from No. 30 top windows', 'excellent soil', 'poor soil' or 'boggy soil', 'potential view from kitchen window', 'keep characterful mature magnolia tree?', 'disguise garage?', etc. This is what I do, and it really helps when coming up with a site-specific design solution and ensures nothing's been left out.

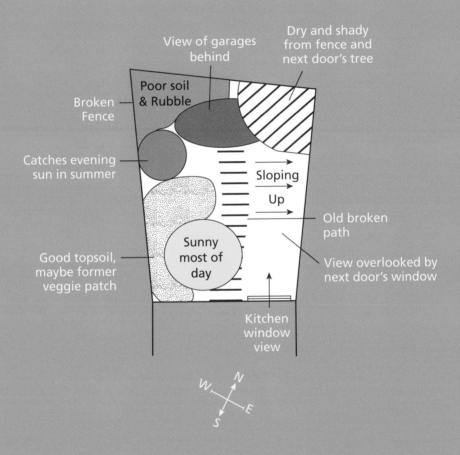

View of garages behind

Dry and shady from fence and next door's tree

Poor soil & Rubble

Broken Fence

Catches evening sun in summer

Sloping

Up

Old broken path

Good topsoil, maybe former veggie patch

Sunny most of day

View overlooked by next door's window

Kitchen window view

N
W   E
S

what is 'aspect'?

The 'aspect' is the way your garden faces, which defines the areas that get plenty of sun and those that are thrown into shadow for all or part of the day. The simplest way to work out your aspect is to stand outside the back wall of your house with a compass or look at a map online and, presuming the garden is relatively square or rectangular, find out which way is south. If south is directly ahead of you then the garden is 'south facing', which means that you will have plenty of sun shining towards the back of the house. Mark this on your sketch and add in north, east and west. In this scenario, your back fence is the 'north-facing' fence, which will be pretty much in shade all day. The left-hand fence will be on the eastern side of the garden and be 'west-facing' and get the afternoon/evening sun. The right-hand fence or wall will be your west fence, which is east-facing and will get some morning sun.

If you have lived in your home for a period of time, you'll probably already have a good understanding of your aspect and the way the sun moves across the garden, throwing certain areas into shade.

Buildings or trees may overshadow your garden and therefore increase shade in certain areas. As you start to build up a profile of the garden, you'll be able to marry these with your brief; for example, if you want a shady seating area there may be an obvious shady place where it would work well, or maybe a priority is to grow sun-loving plants or some edibles, which will require the sunniest spots.

Slopes

Which way your garden slopes (or doesn't) will either increase or negate the amount and spells of shade in the garden. Say the garden is north-facing and the garden slopes down, away from the house, the shade will be increased as a result. Slopes are also a factor when considering the garden layout as the siting and/ or moving of retaining walls and steps to level areas off could have huge implications on moving or excavating large quantities of soil and subsoil. Ideally, any existing soil on site can be cleverly relocated within the garden rather than costing a small fortune to remove and skip (see the levels and steps chapter).

simple solution with corten steel risers and gravel tread!

challenging climates

The climate and aspect of the surrounding area where you live will give you plenty of clues as to what will grow well in your garden. While you assess your aspect, consider the local climatic conditions and how extreme they are. Are you exposed to harsh winds from certain directions? Do you live in a particularly wet or dry part of the country? Coastal areas will be windy, but are often

milder than inland areas, whereas inland areas will be more extreme and tend to get hotter in the summer and colder in the winter. Pockets of microclimates are also created, for example in urban areas, which can significantly change the temperatures, the way the wind works and levels of rainfall, which will ultimately affect your garden and your plants.

Boundaries, surfaces and reclaiming elements

Roughly note any boundaries (including heights) and surfaces (quantities) that you are considering retaining, removing or can possibly be relocated.

Rusty colours tie into the planting with these orange geums.

Soil

Understanding the soil in your garden is extremely important and will certainly determine the plants you can grow. If you have varying areas of good soil and poor soil, this may also be a key factor in the overall layout of your garden. You'll want to make sure the planting areas exploit the good soil and, of course, the hard landscaping areas will work whatever the soil is like underneath so could easily be sited on the poorer areas. Depending on the size of your garden, it's worth testing the soil in various parts rather than just one area as it can vary enormously.

There are six main soil types: clay, sandy, silty, peaty, chalky and loamy. The first thing to do to test your soil is to get your hands in it to feel it and look at it. Rub a small piece, the smoother it is to the touch the more clay content it has and the grittier it is the more sand.

Once you've determined what soil you have it's worth digging a few test holes (it can vary enormously across a garden) to determine its depth and also test the pH with a soil testing kit available from any garden centre. By the time you've done this you'll understand your aspect and soil intimately and the knock-on implications of any design you come up with. There are ways of improving poor soils and you could possibly import some topsoil in certain areas but, as a rule, my advice is to work with what you've got wherever possible.

clay

sandy

silty

peaty

chalky

loamy

Layout

Designing your garden layout is the most important and exciting step. It forms the master plan and direction for any work to be done over the coming weeks, months and years to realise the vision of your dream modern space. With a contemporary garden, a layout plan is perhaps more important than with any other style of garden as it will make it slick, efficient and impactful while dictating material choices, plants and the way it's all put together. This may all sound rather complicated, but is often very simple.

Although a garden will mature and change over the years, the shapes on the ground are the frame on which everything hangs. A drawing will help you see it all and will help you define problem areas in the garden, how it can be connected to the property, key views from inside and, in turn, how to impose some strong and confident shapes to give it that designer edge. You certainly don't need to have any previous drawing or technical experience, just plenty of enthusiasm and be willing to learn. Don't rush it, develop it, walk away and come back to any drawings or sketches several times and play with it on the ground outside until you're sure it's going to look great and function well.

Measure it up and put it on paper

Measuring a site accurately is the key to creating a precise scale site survey and layout drawing that in turn will determine the success of putting your design on the ground. You can't be too precise when measuring and it's often worth taking more measurements than you may

need, which is easy if you are living at the property where the garden is. I always use squared graph paper and draw out the shape of the whole garden on the paper first to make sure it'll fit on one page (A4 is usually sufficient). First, measure the house, marking the dimensions of any windows and doors. If you don't have a long tape measure, use a piece of string with pen marks or bits of tape every metre to measure.

Once you have the house marked, measure up the boundaries. Measure the length of, for example, the side fences and back fence, but never assume that they (or anything in the garden!) are square to the house, even if they look it. Use a simple check system called triangulation that will accurately plot the corners of the garden.

Measure from one corner of the building (called point A) to the far corners of your garden (points X and Y), and then from the other corner of the house (point B) to the same corners (points X and Y). When putting this on paper, you use a compass to scribe the distances and where the two arcs (say, arc A–X and B–X) cross is the true corner of the garden. This triangulation method can be used to plot all the key elements in the garden such as trees, boundaries, existing paving, manholes, etc.

To convert your site survey into a scale drawing back indoors, you'll need graph paper, a pencil, a ruler, a compass and ideally a set square. Work in a scale that fits your paper, so first try to get an idea of how big your garden will be on either A4 or A3 paper first, by measuring out the longest length and width to scale and make sure it fits. I like to work in either 1:50 where 1 cm is equal to 50 cm (half a metre) or 1:100 where 1 cm represents 1 metre. I find 1:100 is the easiest to convert as 5.6 metres will be 5.6 cm on the paper. Once you choose a scale, you must stick to it throughout the whole drawing.

First, plot the building onto your paper, which will also give you points A and B for you to plot your boundaries by using the triangulation method above. This is when you'll need to use your compass to scribe A to X and A to Y, and then B to X and B to Y, and where these compass scribes cross will be the corners of the boundaries. You should double-check these points using the measurements you took of the lengths of the boundaries (as long as they run along a straight line, a taut string line alongside will determine that).

Once you have the site survey to scale, you can start to transpose your concept plan using tracing paper over the top so you can shift things around without rubbing out the survey every time.

Use free software?

There are some free online planning tools like SketchUp that can be used to draw to scale, where it's easy to save and copy files to try and develop ideas. If you are computer savvy, they are easy to learn and I'd recommend having a go. I use them a lot. There are free tutorials online and they can be ideal for simple 3-D modelling, which will give you an excellent idea of how a layout will work, and how it will look from key areas as you move through it.

Drawing a concept layout

Now you have a survey, the fun, creative and practical process of the layout design begins. Drawing up a scale plan will ensure you look in detail at every area before embarking on the construction of the garden. I'd suggest having a read of the other chapters (on surfaces, transitions, boundaries, etc.) before embarking on this, which will help you deliberate about materials, surface shapes and transitions from one surface to the other. Start with surface shapes and also draw in any structures with height too. Even though a pergola structure may not look like a pergola on a plan, it will force solutions such as where the posts are to go, whether they will affect your hard landscaping layout and perhaps ways of getting a nice detail in. Annotate any areas to help you and also add any key dimensions onto the drawing. If it helps, then colour the drawing in too with a match for the possible colours of materials as it will help to give you an idea of whether you've got a good blend and overall balance and proportion of materials to planting. A good garden plan always looks good on paper: balanced, in proportion and flowing.

Designing with materials in mind

As you design, have an idea of what surface materials you may potentially use (see the Surfaces chapter). It's a bit of a chicken and egg situation; you may not know yet, but it's worth having an idea of what will fit into your budget and the kind of surface (paved, gravel, lawn?) needed, as it may affect the shapes you design or, for example, the precise width of a path to avoid the labour and fussy look of cut materials.

mark it on the ground

Once you have an initial plan to work to, get out into the garden and use some string, sticks, hosepipes, builders spray paint, old pots, etc, anything you can get your hands on. Lay it out on the ground to see if it will work and look good. Take a chair out and sit where you've designed seating areas (does it feel comfortable? are you overlooked? do you have a good view?). Stick more canes or sticks in the ground where you may want a large shrub or tree for height to get a real idea three-dimensionally. Walk through the imaginary garden and look 360 degrees around you as you move to imagine what you'll see and imagine where other large plants can go (more sticks or an umbrella taped to a long post?) to break up views or create privacy. This is honestly what I do when on site and then tweak things around till I'm happy and then redraw it accordingly.

tips for designing a modern space

These are my five top tips for designing a great modern space.

1 **Keep it simple, bold and clean**
It's easy to get carried away and overly elaborate with shapes that end up looking fussy and distracting.
The best modern spaces tend to be unfussy, slick and stylish with some strong shapes imposed onto them.
Geometric shapes such as squares, rectangles, circles, arcs, concentric circles, etc. all work well.

Don't be afraid of straight lines! This strong geometry holds the garden together year round.

2 Scale, proportion and balance

Scale and proportion are hard to define. It's the size, and therefore visual weight, of all the elements (landscape materials, structures, plants, etc.) in relation to the human body and the relationship of all those elements to each other. A garden that lacks good scale and proportion will feel awkward, unbalanced and often undesigned; for example, a huge lawn, tiny borders and a long skinny path! I go into more detail in the Surfaces chapter, but a simple grid based on your potential paving size is a particularly easy way to introduce good scale and proportion throughout the garden. Say you're considering a 450 mm x 450 mm paving unit (or whatever it may be), draw a grid on tracing paper (or on your software) and lay it over the survey. Choose and play around with where the grid initially lines up, perhaps in the middle of the back door or window, or from a corner of the building? Working to this grid (shading areas of terraces, planting, paths, etc.) will help to impose scale onto the garden and in turn help with its proportion and overall balance. It'll be practical when constructing, too.

3 Introduce movement

All good gardens have a sense of movement through them; they never feel static. If they're big enough, they pull one through physically to explore and as one moves through it the eye is drawn into areas. When one reaches the end of the garden and turns round or sits, another composition is revealed. The way the layout works and the placing of seating, visual features, boundary treatment and planting all combine to create this all-important 'movement'.

This simple path invites you to take a journey down the garden...

4 Seasonality

Although every garden has peaks and troughs throughout the year, it also has the potential to celebrate every season. In the UK, our temperate climate means we are lucky to have four seasons. Remember, plants not only have flowers, but many other wonderful qualities to embrace including fabulous foliage, coloured and textured bark and stems, fragrance, seed heads, hips, berries and more. If we choose our plants carefully and get them to work hard, we can have something of interest year-round, even in a tiny space.

with considered planting, autumn is a season to look forward to!

5 Versatility

Modern gardens can be particularly flexible and encompass a whole range of functions. When designing, consider carefully what the garden will be used for, by whom and over what kind of time period. A single generous seating area is often more functional than two smaller ones. Children love to play in the garden, but they also grow up very quickly, so rather than turning the garden into a playground, try to design areas that perhaps change function over time.Where space is limited, consider ways of cleverly doubling up areas or elements, such as retaining walls to act as extra seating, adding storage onto the back of a garden studio, etc.).

what to keep and what to lose

Gardens are rarely a blank canvas as we tend to inherit both soft and hard elements when we move into a new plot. When making a successful contemporary garden, everything has to work together, anything that jars or perhaps dominates, taking it in the wrong direction, needs serious consideration on whether it stays, goes or can be altered to fit within the dream scheme. As I often say to my clients and landscapers, 'you can't make an omelette without breaking a few eggs!'.

Does that mean old elements such as old brick or stone walls or even 1970s crazy paving always have to go or be disguised somehow? Certainly not, there are many modern spaces that embrace and incorporate them superbly but only if they sit comfortably and are sited in the right place. Think long and hard about taking out mature, characterful trees and shrubs that have taken years to grow. They will instantly add a sense of age to a garden and are hard to replace. But if you really don't like them for whatever reason then be ruthless, it's your garden. Just because you inherited something, it doesn't mean you have to live with it forever as the new custodian. When I walk into a garden, I can immediately tell what is of value or not and have many clients who, it seems, have waited ages for me to come along and give the blessing to lose something they really didn't like but felt they had to live with forever, because it was already there and the previous owner loved it!

Trees

If you're planning your garden and you decide a tree or two has to go then leave them out of any design going forward (and perhaps the knock-on effects of dry soil and shade beneath). Some trees are simply inappropriate for their setting or growing in the wrong place. Large oaks or eucalyptus, for example, are never going to be a long-term solution in a small garden but on the boundary of a larger garden may provide a fabulous backdrop and privacy from the neighbours too. Some old trees (often fruit trees) may have simply run their course and after many productive years may be on the way out. Most trees, however, are an asset offering seasonal interest in the form of flowers, foliage colour, berries and bark texture. They're great for wildlife too. A mature specimen magnolia, for example, may be fleeting in flower but for a few weeks in spring is simply magical and life-enhancing, oh and the autumn colour is pretty good too!

Some trees benefit hugely from pruning or tree surgery (in the case of larger trees). They can be manipulated to a degree, enhanced, sometimes made to stand proud and sculptural, perhaps worked into a balanced composition or pruned to open up a view (see the connecting to a view chapter).

If a tree has to be felled for whatever reason, I always advocate planting another (more appropriate) tree in the garden. Always use a qualified tree surgeon for larger trees and before touching any tree check whether you're in a conservation area or the tree has a TPO (Tree Preservation Order) on it, which means you'll require permission to do any work on it.

Younger trees that have been planted in the last few years can often be re-sited if dug up and planted carefully at the right time of year (November to March for deciduous and late winter/early spring for evergreens).

shrubs

As we move down the pecking order, shrubs (some are as big as small trees and others smaller bushes) are the next to consider and tend to carry less sentimental value so are easier to lose ,if required. The flower colour tends to be the most contentious issue, so does that bright yellow forsythia work with your colour scheme of whites and pinks or does it slay it? Most tend to flower and are then leafy through summer and many deciduous shrubs put on a good autumnal foliage display that rarely clashes. Again, shrubs can be pruned (you may lose flowers with some for a year depending on pruning time, but most are tough enough and will flower the following year). Depending on their shape, similar to trees they can be thinned, have their crown raised, reduced or perhaps clipped into topiary shapes? Like trees, most can be lifted and moved during the dormant period, especially if they were planted in the last five years or so.

perennials and grasses

Most perennials and grasses are fast growing and relatively cheap to buy, so I never take them into consideration when designing a layout. During a garden build, they can be dug up (and divided at the same time if required) and 'heeled in' for planting later. This is also the time to give away and compost any that simply don't work with your planting scheme. For example, if you're designing a naturalistic border, some exotics and clashing 'glamour queens' will probably have to go or be planted elsewhere in the garden.

structures

Garden structures such as buildings (sheds/studios/ garages), gazebos, pergolas, archways, etc. tend to be quite dominant, so their existing style can dictate the overall character of a garden. Some are simple, others ornate, some frankly hideous! Buildings may be structurally sound and in the right place but does their finish clash with what you're trying to achieve? If so, they potentially could be clad (timber slats/metal sheeting/ painted exterior plyboard, etc.) and even remodelled and re-shaped to help them become more of a contemporary feature or recede into the background. If you want to keep a structure but it's in the wrong place, it can perhaps be resited by dismantling and rebuilding, but it often works out cheaper and easier to get a new one that fits with the new vision. If a gazebo or archway has mature climbers on it, they can often be taken off and laid on the ground while the structure is adapted or replaced. They may need cutting hard back, but most climbers are vigorous and will bounce back.

Surfaces

The garden layout will have taken the above existing elements into consideration, but when it comes to shapes on the ground it's the surfaces that come into play the most. Perhaps you've inherited some valuable materials (granite setts/old brick paviours/natural stone paving) that can be used as part of your plan or added to with extra material (if you can source something similar), or sit nicely alongside a complementary surface material? Measure the precise amount of paving you have and allow for any material that may be unusable or may get broken when lifting.

You may really like an existing material but, once lifted, not have enough to pave a meaningful area? Perhaps incorporate it by edging a path or adding in a detail such as decorative bands in paving and/or bands to delineate paved areas?

Be wary of simply cutting a new shape into an existing area of paving. It usually looks far better working with and considering the qualities of a material first than ending up with something that looks imposed with oddly-shaped cuts around the edges.

It may be a good idea to pressure wash the surface before lifting so it's nice and clean and so that, if supplementing the existing surface with the same type, it may not look too dissimilar (another consideration is, do you mix them up or work in areas?). Most surface materials dull down and weather quite quickly.

solutions for awkward-shaped plots

Good garden design principles can be applied to any garden. I often get asked about creating flowing layouts in awkward-shaped plots and there are some simple tried-and-tested rules and tips that can help turn what is seen as a problematic garden into an exciting space.

Lose the rectangle

Many people inherit a rectangular lawn in a rectangular plot, which is difficult to get away from and does little to create flow and movement. Look to form at least two separate areas with shapes that perhaps overlap and simply flow from one to the other. Between them, leave some space so you can boldly cut into the garden with planting areas so you can introduce some taller plants into the central space to break it up. Visually, losing the boundaries will make the garden feel bigger and take the emphasis away from the rectangle, so plant them up with climbers. A diagonal axis is a fine way to break up a rectangular plot, so rather than having paved areas or lawns running parallel to the boundaries, try setting them at an angle, which immediately changes the shape of the surrounding planting areas and loses that rectangle.

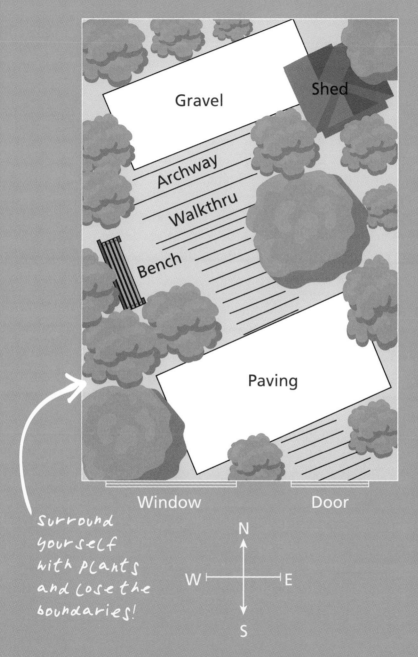

Gravel

Shed

Archway

Walkthru

Bench

Paving

Window

Door

surround
yourself
with plants
and lose the
boundaries!

N

W ⊢────────⊣ E

S

shallow but wide garden

Ideally, the design screens off the shorter boundary immediately in front of you as you enter the garden, tricking the eye into not knowing precisely where the short view of the garden ends, and encourages one to turn towards the longer view by drawing the eye and initiating movement towards the journey. A feature pot or sculpture left unobscured and placed in the far corner could help to do this. This turn will make the garden feel bigger and introduce the all-important movement too. As with all gardens, it's important to have a destination point to head for – in this case, a seat – framed by a generous and inviting wide arch that emphasises the garden's width. With the planting, it's important to put some taller plants along the house side too so that it feels balanced as you look down it.

Triangular plot

If it's a large triangle, then there may be a way of dividing it into rooms, but with a small triangular plot, it's better to keep it as one simple space. Imposing a strong geometrical shape, such as a brick or gravel circle, will help to lose the strange shape, giving it an internal courtyard feel. Any areas outside the new circle can be turned into planting areas, and any paths or seating areas that work off it look best radiating out from the circle's central point. By infilling the new planting areas, it won't feel awkward any more.

This bold feature closes the garden's dark corner behind it.

Long, thin garden

The common mistake with long, thin gardens is to have the central areas wide open (like the Great British Classic 'lawn in the middle') so you look straight down the garden to the back fence, which emphasises its shape and the design lacks any sense of intrigue or movement. These are crying out to be divided into 'rooms' so one gets the sense they are really moving through the garden to a destination point at the end. The 'diagonal approach' outlined in 'Lose the rectangle' above works well and can perhaps be repeated so it fits the length of the garden nicely. Another approach may be to make a more contemporary formal garden with rooms based on a symmetrical layout, but you'll have to love formal gardens to live with one!

This simple, meandering path creates easy flow and balanced, generous planting areas on either side.

formality

Modern formal gardens can be stunning. We all admire and like to walk through formal gardens, but perhaps you need to be a certain type of person to want to create, live with and garden in one. Someone who loves everything neat and tidy at all times? If you have a large space to play with then it's possible you could have both formal and informal areas, introducing some formality around the house with a looser feel further away, but if the plot isn't huge then my advice is to go with either one or the other.

Some sites cry out for a formal approach. Square courtyards and walled spaces work particularly well. If the back of the house has a symmetrical elevation with the door in the middle and the windows balanced either side, then this could be a fine starting point. The movement of a formal garden will often have a very 'up and down' feel with a strong line of symmetry, so the garden plan could be folded in half (and half again?) and then the two halves or four quarters would be the same. On the ground, this may need a tweak or two, but it's paramount that when your eye is drawn towards a key view it's not disappointed when it gets there, so the choice and placing of any sculpture or feature plants can make or break it. A formal courtyard may look best with a large central feature off which everything else hangs, as this internalises the space, always drawing the eye into the centre and away from the boundaries.

If you do choose a formal layout, you don't always have to follow it religiously with the planting of the garden. In fact, a degree of formal with a few key evergreens or topiary pieces creates a strong year-round framework for a more relaxed perennial style to erupt through and around it in spring and summer. The underlying structure is revealed once again through the dormant months.

If the back garden isn't the place to make a formal garden, then perhaps your front garden is, if you have one. This is especially so if the front door and gate are central and line up. They can look superb, balance the architecture of a symmetrical building, draw it down and tie it into the landscape nicely.

transitions and edges

Well-designed modern gardens have areas and level changes that dovetail together like a hand-crafted jigsaw, and these 'transitions' are not solely about the aesthetics of a space but are enormously practical too. Paying attention to them early on will make your garden feel slick and help it flow nicely. Ignoring them or dealing with them when they crop up often leads to issues down the line in construction or, even worse, stand out as an obvious oversight!

As one transitions from one area to another, the drama can be increased. An obvious change in the surface material perhaps? Squeezing and narrowing the dimensions of a crossover between areas increases anticipation of what's beyond and two vastly different styles of planting each side of the transition will mark the distinction. In contrast, the changes can be very subtle and fluid: the surface material varying slightly or even staying the same, the access generous and inviting or the planting palette very similar with delicate changes on each side.

paving edge

Surfaces constructed in units (such as timber, paving or brick paviours) will ideally end on a full unit rather than a fiddly cut, which will always look like an afterthought. Measure it out carefully before laying. This edge will determine where and how the next surface or planting area will butt up to it. Subtle contrasts, such as using the same material for the next area but changing the dimension or direction in which it is laid, can work really well too. Even putting a 'band' of another material in between will define one area from another. The level of the next material needs considering too. Planting areas should ideally be a little lower to stop soil spillage or they may need some kind of retainer. Other walking surfaces should be as flush as possible to avoid a trip step, whereas lawns should be set a little lower (see below) for mowing.

Lawn edging

Many gardens have a 'soft' lawn edge that requires preserving (edging and cutting regularly with a half-moon tool). They are fine and cost nothing initially, but a lawn can often morph into an amoebic shape over time (cutting round a plant here and there or going a bit freeform with the edger!). A permanent lawn edge will define its shape and reduce maintenance hugely, working as a mowing edge and removing the need to get out the edging shears or strimmer altogether. If an area needs re-seeding or turfing, the edge is already there to work to.

Brick paviours, granite setts, timber (gravel boards or railway sleepers) or metal products (specifically designed for lawn edging and can be bent into arcs) are all good choices. Which you go for will depend on budget and how they work with the other materials in your garden. Set any mowing edge just below the lawn level (around 10–20 mm) so that when mowing you can simply mow over it. Transitions between any paved surfaces that meet a lawn are ideally set at this level too, so they are easy to walk between and mow over. Paths around a lawn can double up really well as an edge, with the lawn on one side and plants billowing over the path's edge on the other.

From gravel to hard surface

Loose materials, such as gravel, usually require an edge to contain the material and define its shape. Gravel butting up to lawn will require an edge, whereas when transitioning onto paving, the paving material acts as an edge itself. It's then just a case of getting the levels correct so that the gravel doesn't spill.

Bleeding areas together

A harsh 'one thing or another' edge may feel just too abrupt. A clever yet simple way to make a transition feel more sinuous is to 'bleed' and dissipate one material into another. It's a lot easier to do with one hard material (paving) and one loose (lawn or gravel), perhaps having stepping stones running off the edge of a solid paved area. Always place the paving first to check it not only looks good but is practical to step between too.

This is a famous Japanese moss garden. The balance between nature and man-made materials are in pure harmony

planting areas

Your planting areas may be clearly defined and contained by the hard landscape areas or retaining walls. Again, there are ways of 'bleeding' plants into the hard landscaped areas to soften those junctions and help the planting feel as if it's flowing and spilling through the garden rather than harnessed within a defined space. Planting into gravel areas is easy. Leaving paving slabs out to create these planting opportunities can look superb but needs consideration as part of the layout plan rather than lifting slabs or placing pots as an afterthought.

hard
landscaping

surfaces

Some may turn off when they hear the term 'hard landscaping', but as a one-time landscaper turned designer, a wonderful wall, set of steps or section of paving can get me quite excited! These elements don't have to be fancy (far from it), design is all about understanding space and suitable materials to create something greater than the sum of its parts.

In a modern space, the hard elements should complement each other and slot together like a beautifully crafted piece of furniture. Design, planning and attention to detail are, therefore, paramount.

Rather than simply 'slabbing' an area over, consider your options before it's too late. Budget is a key consideration of course; surfaces vary hugely in price depending on the site, material chosen and installation techniques.

Look to incorporate areas for planting wherever possible to soften edges and make terraces and patios feel as if they're within the garden rather than an add-on. It is a chicken-and-egg situation when designing the layout as some materials and dimensions are better suited to certain shapes, and larger paving units (without expensive and fiddly cutting!) will determine sizes such as the width of paths and terraces.

I usually limit surfaces in a contemporary garden to a maximum of two (that complement each other) otherwise they can look a little fussy.

Get an idea of cost

Once you have an idea of shapes, you'll be able to measure and get an approximate quantity of square metre cover of surfaces. If you're a DIY type like me (come on, I know there's some out there!) you can work out costs yourself. If not, get a good local landscaper and ask them for an idea of cost for different materials (see below); they may be able to help with suppliers, get a good deal and advise on the next stage of installation too. You'll already be ahead of the game and know roughly what you want, which is always a good thing. Discuss other associated costs too, such as any excavation or drainage work. Some materials (deck, gravels etc.) freely drain through whereas most hard paving (stone/ brick paviours etc.) will require somewhere for the rain to run off, particularly relevant when near the house. The costs are likely to dictate what you can or can't afford. As a result, perhaps one area can be a lovely cut stone, offset by the path and the rear seating area can be in a cheaper material such as self-binding gravel. Or perhaps you can spread costs: do one area this year and another next, all part of the master plan for a great garden in the long term.

Finesse and finalise the design using the chosen material

Now we know the rough shapes and materials, we can get down to detailing, and the more detailed the better, even drawing out an entire paving plan, every brick, or every slab ideally. Think about the directions of the way they are laid and the joints, and whether that speeds up or slows down the eye as you look along or across it.

choices of materials and their pros and cons

There are ethical considerations with many materials (hardwood decks, stone's source of origin, etc.) to research before buying.

Decking (softwood or hardwood)
Pros: Soft, quiet, warm. Easy and quick to install (perhaps DIY?) and ideal for floating over tricky uneven areas and slopes.

Cons: Poor quality decks don't last too long. They can look rather as if they have been plonked down if not thought through.

Tip: If it's grooved one side and smooth the other, use the smooth side face-up. The grooves often fill up with debris and get slippery (pressure wash them if they do).

Real stone paving (such as Yorkstone, sandstone, basalt, granite, quartzite, porphyry)
Pros: Creates a sense of permanence, natural colour tones, many look great when wet.

Cons: Expensive, requires skill to lay and requires a sub-base. Usually requires excavation.

Tip: In a modern space, these materials tend to look best laid in grids or in courses (lines of the same sizes like bricks). Random sizes are harder to lay and will give a more traditional look.

Composite and concrete paving
Pros: Cheaper than real stone. Even thickness and standard sizing, which means it's quicker to lay.

Cons: Many composites mimic real stone but lack the depth of texture and colour.

Tip: With large areas of paving, try to soften with plenty of plants, from planting pockets within larger areas and/ or combining in the next, to a more textured surface such as gravel.

Crazy paving
Pros: Far cheaper to buy than rectangular paving (often sold in weight) whether it's natural or concrete and can look great in contemporary gardens if well executed.

Cons: Needs laying really well to look good. Large expanses can look a little fussy and dated.

Tip: The larger the pieces the better and the pointing (grouting in paving) will make or break it.

Brick, paviours and granite setts
Pros: Smaller units, so ideal for intimate spaces, courtyards, front gardens etc. Versatile. Work well in many different patterns (basketweave, herringbone, stretcher bond) and can be laid on curves and arcs.

Cons: Avoid using in large areas as can look a little municipal. Setts can be a little uneven for seating areas.

Tip: Laying courses across the garden will slow down the eye and laying them lengthways (along paths to a feature perhaps?) will draw and speed it up.

Gravel, chippings, self-binding gravels and other loose aggregates

Pros: Very quick to install, buy in bags or loose and simply place onto a pinned fabric and rake out. Self-binding gravels can quickly be consolidated with a wacker plate. Can be planted through. Forms great textures.

Cons: Loose materials can get kicked around and pick up dirt. Not great for family gardens with kids.

Tip: Will need some sort of edge such as timber, brick or bent steel to retain and can help with a designer look. Larger aggregates, around 20 mm, stay in place better and cats don't use them as a tray!

Resin-bonded aggregates

Pros: Can form a smooth surface with a relatively natural look depending on colour chosen (wide range). Ideal for wheelchairs and those with accessibility issues. Free draining.

Cons: Needs specialist installation and quite expensive.

boundaries

Garden boundaries delineate your space and create privacy and tend to be the first constructed element that goes into a complete garden redesign. You may have inherited some great boundaries (even with old and traditional you can see what to keep and what to lose) that you can incorporate or adapt to work with your modern vision and perhaps take some clues from them when it comes to material choice and detailing in other areas of the garden. Boundaries are often seen as mostly functional but, from a design perspective, their aesthetics play a large part too. They can be very subtle or even visually non-existent, helping the garden to recede into the distance or connect with a view beyond, but in smaller spaces they internalise the garden, come to the fore and can dictate the overall feel of it.

Fencing

fence panels

hit and miss

louvred panels

custom design

colours
see paint, stain and
colour chapter

Hedges (see Plants and hedges below)

We don't plant enough hedges, often opting for a quick-fix solution. They are great for wildlife and in windy areas filter the wind rather than creating damaging eddies on the garden side. They can add a lovely texture and change with the seasons too so are well worth considering for a contemporary garden. Sure, they need some regular maintenance, but they quickly become part of the green architecture of a garden, adding volume and a softness that is impossible to find with building materials. They tend to be clipped square along the top, but try to think outside the box. I've seen some fabulous hedges that are more organic in shape, perhaps with soft curves and waves that tie into the view or help get away from the rectangular shape of the garden rather than reinforce it.

imagine this corner of the garden with a bare fence? way too harsh!

walling

A beautiful brick or stone wall adds a sense of permanence to a garden and warms up and retains heat well for growing a host of plants in front of it. Building walls is quite involved as excavations and foundations need to go in. A high-quality bespoke fence may be less expensive than a wall made from cheap materials, so consider your options. A lower wall with some trellising on top is a way of keeping height and reducing costs.

Brick walls: The main design consideration with brick walls is the choice of brick (does the house brick or stone colour give any clues to match or complement it with?) and the type of bond used. There are many types of bonds and details (such as piers and coping) to consider but a good local bricklayer should be able to help.

A beautiful brick wall like this adds character, so at least some should be seen!

Block rendered walls: Concrete block walls require foundations but are one of the most economical options around for a solid structure.

Stone walls: In a rural setting, a beautifully crafted stone wall can add a huge amount of character, sense of permanence and, if made in local stone, will connect it to the local landscape too. Stone walling is all about quality workmanship and finishing.

Stone cladding: This may conjure up some horrific images of houses in the 1970s but there are some fine tile-like modular stone products on the market in a range of finishes that are fixed onto block walls and work out cheaper than solid stone. I've recently used one on a project and it looks great.

green them up with climbers

There is no point in spending a large proportion of your budget on boundaries if you're planning on covering them in climbers so that in time they won't be seen at all. On the other hand, some climbers are an ideal and economic way to hide ugly or incongruous or inconsistent boundaries, to green them up and bring them together (see 'climbers' in the plants directory).

paths

I sometimes come away from a garden feeling frustrated with the lack of path love. An otherwise fab garden let down with a predictable A-to-B path which, with a little imagination, could have contributed a lot more. Most paths are viewed as being practical to keep feet, barrows and kids off planting areas (and lawns when wet) but in a modern space where aesthetics are important it has the potential to become a thing of beauty. Planning is key. Consider its route, size, material choice, relationship to the other elements and how to plant in or around it.

path siting

A path right up the middle of a garden will split it in two, drawing the eye right up the centre. This may work in a strict formal layout, but most of us want an informal space, so the path becomes a restricting, dare I say it, disastrous choice, hindering the chance of any flow. It also limits what you can do either side of it. Straight paths off to one side or the other, running parallel with the fence line create a similar 'up and down' effect and similarly feel too obvious.

When it comes to path lines, there's a happy balance between the all-important movement through a garden and human behaviour. Over-elaborate twists and turns will make one feel manipulated and fight against a natural 'desire line'; corners will be cut. A desire line is the way one would naturally walk through the plot if there were no paths at all; it's often a gentle meander and could help determine your ideal line. Lay hosepipe out on the ground during the layout design stage to visualise how this may work and what areas would be left either side for lawn, seating areas, planting areas, etc. Another easy technique is to take a photo on a tablet on a wide shot and draw over it with different path lines and shapes, then try these on the ground to see how they are to walk upon.

path widths

There are no set rules. A narrow path will limit it to one person walking along it at a time but too narrow and it may feel uninviting. For two people to walk side-by-side, allow a minimum of 1.5 metres. Be as generous as possible so that plants can flop over and soften the edges without impinging on the path itself. Consider widening the path a little in key areas so a large pot (as an eye catcher) or bench (as a pause in the design and spot to rest) can be placed strategically to one side while the path carries on. This will help break it up, make it feel less like a track and more of an intrinsic part of the garden.

This bench makes a great focal and destination point. The path around it is generous and welcoming.

Materials

Once you have an idea of direction, shape and width, you can consider what material(s) work best without a new path looking like an add-on. If there's a way of using one of the surface materials already in your garden (terrace/patio) or combining it with another it will help bring the garden style together cohesively. Say the terrace is in brick or paviour, perhaps line the path with the same or, if it's stone, continue the material effortlessly through into the path. As with all surfaces, unit size is important too, especially if you want smooth curves. Small units such as paving setts or bricks can be fanned out or laid in arcs. I would rather keep large individual paving slabs as pure rectangles because a cut curved edge is not only tricky to do but looks a little enforced. Large units can work well for meandering paths but will need to be gently staggered/offset.

Direction

The direction in which the material is laid can make a subtle difference too. Lining bricks lengthways towards the long view will draw the eye quickly along it (towards a sculpture perhaps?) but if they run across the garden sideways or at an angle, this will slow the eye down, which works well in a small space. Loose materials like chippings, gravel or self-binding gravel (which when compacted makes a smooth surface) are good value and work well for all sorts of shapes. I like the way they can be planted into for a natural look; in effect, the path then becomes the area where the plants are left out.

This path laid across the view slows the eye down nicely.

path edges

Ideally, paths are set just above the level of a flower bed to stop soil spillage and just below a lawn so the mower can cleanly run over the path without the need for getting the lawn edger out. It may mean a little digging out or perhaps putting a step in, but it's well worth the effort as it looks crisp and reduces maintenance in the long term. Gravel and aggregates will need a retaining edge whether that is treated timber boards, brick or granite setts, or off-the-peg interlocking steel edging that comes in sections and can be bent into soft curves.

perfect height for mowing straight over!

planting

The planting either side or in the middle of a path (if you've left some gaps) will either help soften it and sit into the garden comfortably or, in the case of hedges, accentuate and bring out the dynamic line of it. Here are some fine plants to do this job.

Good plants for breaking edges of paths:

Stachys byzantina (sunny spot, soft silvery foliage)

Persicaria amplexicaulis 'Firetail'

Low grasses (e.g. *Hakonechloa macra* in semi-shade)

Hardy geraniums (geranium 'Rozanne')

Good plants for gaps in paths to soften them

Alchemilla mollis (lady's mantle)
or the smaller *alchemilla erythropoda*

Creeping thyme – lots of forms

Chamomile 'Treneague'

Corsican mint

Hedging plants alongside paths

Lavender

Pittosporum tobira 'Nanum' (informal mounds)

Hebe rakaiensis (informal mound)

Box (formal)

Lonicera nitida

Ilex crenata

Levels and steps

At garden design college, some students would freak out when levels and slopes were mentioned and when we measured up plots that weren't perfectly flat. I had plenty of construction experience beforehand, which helped, and now prefer designing gently sloping gardens over flat ones. Level changes create the opportunity to introduce extra interest, movement and direction through architectural elements such as terraces, steps and retaining walls and these can be left exposed or part softened with planting.

If a garden is already flat, I sometimes introduce simple level changes for the same reasons, and they can also be a clever way of significantly keeping costs down and creating a greener solution. Spoil from any excavations for wall foundations, paved areas or ponds can often be redistributed on the site to introduce a level change rather than being skipped and carted off for landfill, which can escalate costs.

Extremely sloping gardens can undeniably be a real challenge, especially if space is confined. They can be tricky to design and tricky to build. More often than not the solution incorporates structural walls, knee-aching steps and view-blocking balustrades. As well as the visual and practical problems, they can be prohibitively expensive too!

If you do have a slope, the first thing to do is to get an overview of precisely what you're dealing with. Here's my low-tech guide to working out your slope. You'll need a long stick, a spirit level, some string, a tape measure and, ideally, a willing helper.

Ask your friend to stand at the lowest point of the garden with the long stick. Tie the string round it in a loop so it can be moved up or down. Leave them at the bottom, and head to the highest point in the garden with the other end of the string. Put a peg into the ground at the highest point, so it's nice and firm, and tie the string off so it's touching the ground (if it's paving, tie it to a brick or two to weigh it down). Then head back to the bottom, stretch the string tight at the lower end and move it up and down the long stick till it's perfectly level by holding the spirit level carefully along the string. When it's level (bubble in the middle), measure down from the string to the ground. Hey presto! This will give you the overall height difference of your garden. You can do this for the slope between any two key points if you want and for large gardens or super-steep gardens, do it in sections. So now you can start to make some simple calculations and think about any implications they will have with regard to level changes, steps and any retaining walls.

Steps

Let's say the height difference in your garden from your calculation above is 120 cm (or 1.2 m). With steps, you're looking at ideally 15 cm per step riser (although anything between 12.5 cm and 20 cm is acceptable), so you'll need eight steps of 15 cm (8 x 15 = 120) to get from the bottom to the top to take the slope out completely. Perhaps you want your garden split into three main, level, terraced areas with the first being the bottom level, four steps to the second and another four to the top? Or two steps to the second and then six to the top?

The tread (the flat bit you put your foot on) should be at least double the riser, but if you have the room then make this generous and easy to stride with two paces per tread. Try the spacing out before building as anything caught between the two may lead to an annoying half skip when walking!

But garden steps are just steps, right? Well, I would argue that they can make or break your garden and, being a key construction element, have the potential to be beautiful and elegant. At best, they can tempt you to dance up and down them (like Fred Astaire and Ginger Rogers), and, at worst, they can be dangerous. Poorly designed steps can create a psychological barrier and

can split a garden (not good) rather than linking areas together.

There are three main things to remember when designing and building steps: (1) Where are they placed in the garden? (2) how and from what are they built? (3) how are they tied into any walling or terracing?

Precisely where they go will dictate the way you want to move through the garden and will have a huge knock-on effect on the garden's layout and the way you move through it. Lining them all up in a straight line may seem the simplest solution but will produce a straight-line path, whether it's on one side of the garden or the other, or even straight up the middle. This leads to an A-to-B path and possibly a formal layout. Consider offsetting them by, say, placing the first set towards the left-hand garden side (lining up with the back door?) and the second on the right or vice versa, possibly set at an angle to the house, or incorporate a twist into the step design too. Don't force it if it doesn't work, but this

what we call 'lazy steps'! They're very easy and flow nicely.

approach could add a key flow and informality to the garden and mean that you walk through and use the whole of the garden space, rather than just heading up and down one side all the time.

When it comes to choosing materials, I tend to look to use either the same material as the paving or a complementary material, and stick to the same unit size or a division or multiple of that size. For example, if I were using a 60 cm x 60 cm paving unit, 60 cm x 30 cm paving slabs for steps would fit into the plan layout, be easy to build and introduce simple continuity to the garden. Although they are a feature, if they are built in a completely different material, they may shout out and feel like an addition. Construction can get expensive too as they usually need concrete foundations, but the simple

Nestled into the landscape with fab planting!

construction of railway sleepers used as a riser infilled with gravel behind for treads will keep both material and labour costs down, but may look too chunky for some gardens.

Wherever steps go, walls will usually be built too as the soil on each side will need to be retained to stop the bank from collapsing and spilling soil on your steps. This is where you can start to get clever by integrating the steps and walling together, which in turn can help drive a particular garden style. Plants can help to soften these junctures by spilling over the edges. I always look for ways that steps and integrated walling can increase the usability of the garden too and, where space is limited, perhaps they can double up as extra seating just by throwing a few cushions around.

furniture

Good quality, well-designed garden furniture can get
seriously expensive, but it can visually 'upgrade' a pretty
average-looking garden. On the other, hand cheap-
looking furniture will have precisely the opposite effect
and often be the first place the critical eye comes to rest,
especially in a small garden. There are literally hundreds
of different types and styles available to buy, some
entirely wood or some a combination of wood and metal,
such as lightweight aluminium. Other materials include
woven rattan and wicker, synthetic woven materials,
plastic and acrylics. If you are creating a contemporary
garden, avoid introducing traditional furniture and
look for a style that will work with the garden as a
whole. Seriously mad bright colours may have seemed
like a good idea at the time ... whereas stark white
garden furniture is best avoided too as it's an extremely
demanding colour and rarely complements any other
structures or planting.

Dining tables and chairs

Some small gardens have been
completely designed around a
main table and a set of chairs
to create the ultimate 'outdoor
dining room' for al fresco
dining. As with interior tables,
consider extendable tables to
give you increased flexibility,
and round tables work well
where space may be squeezed.

sofas

With the demand for comfort, there are now many stylish yet slouchy outdoor sofas similar to interior furniture, some complete with shower-proof cushions. They

often come in modules that can be easily changed to give variety and flexibility to a party garden. Think carefully before purchasing though as they do tend to be bulky items that dominate a space, and please don't forget to measure and work out how you're actually going to get them into the garden before you buy (either through the house or down a side alley). Yes ... it has been known for them not to make it!

steamers and loungers

These can give you a nautical flavour and tend to be for those who take their relaxation as

horizontally as possible or are total sun worshippers. They do take up a surprising amount of ground space when laid out on the ground and can be tricky to store.

Benches

I love a great bench. They can help to define and hold a particular area of the garden together all by themselves when placed alone, say under a tree in the shade or onto a planted gravel surface, and can make it an inviting destination point. See it as an opportunity to add in a more sculptural element and remember, a great bench will last you a lifetime so they're worth investing in.

Built-in

Built-in furniture can work extremely well in a garden as it will become a strong and permanent visual feature, especially when built out of complementary or matching materials such as timber and rendered blockwork to fully integrate it. This is also an efficient use of space if any retaining walls are to be built, as they can form the back of the bench too. An L-shaped bench works well where space is particularly limited and makes for a sociable set-up and an additional dining or coffee table and a few chairs can be brought out when needed to complete the arrangement. Make sure to get the size and height of the actual seat and back right by measuring other furniture you particularly like. The big consideration with built-in seating is how comfortable it ends up, as they tend to be made of rather harsh materials to last, so when designing it consider and allow, height-wise, for having fitted cushions made up to size to complete the look or to bring plenty of cushions outdoors from inside when needed.

café style

Many of the garden centres, interior furniture shops, and even hardware stores now sell a range of foldable, café-style tables and chairs that are ideal for tiny  gardens and balconies for breakfasting in a sunny spot, or where you want to be able to add to existing seating to increase the number of people you can entertain. These can often be stored on a wall on simple brackets.

Hammocks

There is nothing better than relaxing and swinging in a hammock under the shade of a tree on a hot summer's day. Some come with frames, some will require strong fixings into walls or can be tied around mature trees. The ones without frames can easily be rolled up and stored for the winter, so consider whether you want a hammock frame taking up a large chunk of your garden all year round. I love lounging in the fine Mexican-style hammocks that you lie in sideways. The larger ones can take the whole family, though there is a technique to be mastered for getting in and out of them! They need more space than you think, around 3.5–4 metres in length between fixings.

connecting to a view

Some gardens have good views, some have fabulous views. Perhaps you're lucky enough to have a garden that looks out onto a bucolic scene of rolling fields or mature woodland or you have a coastal garden with glimpses of the sea? Or maybe it's a city space with a peek of an iconic building over the boundary wall? Views add a pivotal dimension and consideration when making a garden but open up a possibility to end up with something particularly special too.

A view of a natural landscape beyond your garden boundaries should always be respected; ignore it at your peril. It was there before your garden was made and is likely to be there long after. Be sensitive and try to conjure up a garden with a strong 'sense of place'; one that feels as if it's been waiting for you to come along and mould it from the earth. But can a rural garden with a view be a modern space? Yes, and many fabulous ones are. Just as contemporary architecture can sit superbly in a country setting, so can a fine modern garden.

Layout

There are likely to be key spots that the panorama is best viewed from. Perhaps the light changes across the day and with it the best viewing angle? One spot for the morning and one for the afternoon? These are areas to be exploited, to sit, relish and spend time in. If you're taking over a new property, don't rush into any decisions as views can change significantly from season to season. When sketching your site analysis, add in these key factors too, which will determine your garden layout.

Looking for clues

with a view like that, you simply can't compete!

Connecting a garden to its setting is all about embracing what is already there and not fighting it. Look for clues such as colours in the bark, and the dominant hues in the leaves of trees and plants beyond (that can be picked up in your planting). Is that heather on the side of the hill in the distance? What hedges can you see? Beech, hawthorn, blackthorn? These may be plants you can use in your garden design or mimic with other garden plants to link the two together.

shapes

Modern gardens don't always have to be rectilinear and work from the lines of the house outwards. The shapes of fields, or the profile of a hill in the distance can be picked up on and gracefully linked into the shapes of the garden whether it's paved areas, paths, hedging, planting areas, etc. Play around with shapes (on the ground with hosepipes and string or take pics and sketch over) to connect with the dominant lines of the landscape.

Choosing and losing plants

Plants play a key role in all gardens but choosing a plant palette for a garden with a connection to a wider landscape is critical to its success. You will have to be pretty ruthless with plant choice, which I'm afraid may mean rejecting some of your favourite plants if they don't fit in with the bigger picture. Work the other way around and look for plants that sit comfortably with what's already there.

- **Deciduous trees** (perhaps with characterful multi-stemmed shapes) that offer up good autumn colours to tie in with the trees beyond.

- **Grasses** introduce a long-lasting naturalistic element to reflect the seasons subtly and can have bulbs planted between them to naturalise. They are pretty low maintenance and work well with many perennials too. Whether using short or tall varieties, plant in large bold swathes.

- **Wildflower meadows** don't have to be huge areas and can be excellent temporary solutions for areas you're looking to plant up more permanently in future. There are both annual or perennial seed mixes in a range of colours or mix your own.

- **Bulbs that naturalise:** Think of plants like camassias, alliums, narcissi, etc. and plant them in quantity.

- **Clipped shapes and hedge lines:** Topiary shapes don't have to be balls, cubes or squirrels! Organic mounded shapes and waves may tie in well with the views beyond. You may have some existing shrubs or hedges that are crying out to be clipped into shapes that'll work nicely.

- **Plants with small leaves** keep the eye moving along and lead the eye into the distance. I would avoid plants with large or glossy leaves (laurel and photinia hedges) which tend to stand out and foreshorten the view.

- Don't be sentimental, lose any plants that just don't work in the setting.

- Be careful with glamour queens (bright colours, big and blousy flowers) as they're demanding on the eye. If you have to have them, perhaps plant them out of the key views.

- Be careful with exotic aliens. Large-leafed or unusual plants rarely look comfortable alongside a wider setting.

Framing a view

Within a view, you may want to screen a part of it (where you can see a road or buildings) to help draw the eye towards the best part of it or create some foreground to neatly frame the composition. There are no set rules, but these are the considerations I would take when choosing how to do it.

Balance: Using the same tree or large shrub either side of a view will draw the eye through the gap and forms a strong sense of formality. Would this work with the garden as a whole or perhaps something looser? Two (or more) different trees can work really well for framing, but they should feel balanced in height and form and relate to each other regardless of the view.

Deciduous or evergreen: Evergreen trees are limited in choice but give year-round cover. Once a deciduous tree drops its leaves, its tracery of branches may still give enough cover.

Structures: Trees take years to mature (no reason for not planting one!) but you could frame a view using a structure such as an archway or pergola to look through. This could create a classic picture frame view, like looking through a window. Independent structures either side without a crossbeam will do a similar job without cutting across the view, which may work better depending on where you're standing or sitting.

opening up a view

You may have a fabulous view obscured by a tree, large shrub or overgrown hedge. It may ultimately need to be taken out altogether to open up the view but there are ways of pruning or having tree surgery done that may create foreground and save the plants.

- **Raising the crown:** This is where the lower branches are taken off, revealing more of the main stem or trunk (which can be a major asset in itself). The plant may be tall enough to take enough branches off to see the view (especially when seated).

- **Thinning:** This is taking out, say, one-third of branches to lighten the canopy. During this process, some branches or stems could be selectively taken out or shortened to open up the view without ruining the balance of the plant or tree.

- **Reducing:** Taking off some of the height of a plant or hedge, perhaps to see over the top of it from a raised seating area? Hedges can usually cope with being cut hard back. Most trees and shrubs can be reduced but this often results in encouraging vigorous re-growth, so once done may need to be done on a regular basis.

open boundaries

Boundaries may demarcate your property, but they can also be a visual barrier or distract from the view. Can you lose them altogether? This means your garden looks as if it never ends and you can pretend you own as far as the eye can see! If you need to keep a physical boundary, there are solutions (such as a simple post and wire fence) that are a lot less intrusive than a solid or even 'hit and miss' style picket fence. A ha-ha ditch may sound very grand, but they were invented just for this purpose, to be a vertical and physical barrier to provide uninterrupted views of the landscape beyond (and to stop livestock eating your garden!).

features

Placing an eye-catching ornament

Garden ornaments such as sculptures, large pots and stand-alone water features can help style a garden and draw the eye into key areas or along lengthy views. Garden ornaments are an extremely personal thing, like the pictures in your house, so could perhaps be sentimental or a spur-of-the-moment purchase. I can't help you choose them, but my advice is to not overfill the garden with ornaments as it can become distracting. One or two well-placed and well-chosen ones integrated into the space can work really well. Consider their size and height in relation to the overall scale of the garden. Their placing is what will help them to sit comfortably in the garden and may make or break whether they work well or not. Don't just plonk – those who plonk are plonkers!

This plinth is the perfect height, and the dark yew behind is the perfect foil!

Types of ornament

Water features: Moving water adds movement and often sound so can animate and cool a garden on a hot summer day. Off-the-peg water features tend to be wall-mounted or stand-alone. For the pump to recirculate, it will require a (hidden) power source. They need quite a bit of maintenance, topping up in summer and the occasional clean.

Sculpture: I'm a little wary when a client says they have a sculpture they'd like to display in the garden! There's such a huge range of styles and prices (from mass-produced to serious art pieces in masses of finishes). The best add character and interest without dominating.

Pots: A beautiful feature pot or container can look stunning and may be the way to go if you want something sculptural but not a 'sculpture' as such. Containers are commonly found in gardens so work in context and look good without any plants in them at all.

Driftwood, reclaimed elements, etc: You may have found (or made) something that you want to place in the garden. The trick is to make it look intentional and planned (see previous page).

Now that's a big planter! I love (subtle) humour in a garden, and this makes me chuckle.

placing an ornament

- For stand-alone pieces, a simple backdrop of textural (perhaps evergreen?) foliage or placing nestled next to the trunk of a tree will help anchor it visually and balance it out.

- Don't necessarily place on the ground, consider bringing it up to eye level. If it's small, low down and getting lost, consider raising it on a simple plinth or block of wood.

- For wall-mounted pieces and water features, check the height before fixing. Walk around and view it from different angles. Consider growing a climber or two either side to break up the edges and help nestle it into the planting.

- Avoid placing a sculpture slap bang in the middle of a garden unless it's a showcase centrepiece or as part of a formal garden or a courtyard.

- Consider placing the sculpture further back into a planting area with a little foreground of light planting to soften it so it's not so obvious.

- If your garden is divided into separate areas, perhaps place a piece to draw the eye from one area to the other, encouraging you to explore the garden.

- Place at the end of a long path to maximise the long view.

paint, stain and colour

The Romans loved their painted frescos and trompe-l'œil
has been executed to full trickery effect since the ancient
Greeks first started it. More recently (well, last century)
the contrasting and colourful work by the late Mexican
architect Luis Barragán showed how vibrant colours
can look great in both architecture and the landscape.
Barragán painted entire walls with single primary colours,
often contrasting with walls of brash pinks, oranges and
purples.

Painted backdrops intensify the hues of the plants
in front, especially mid and dark greens, but will also
set off flower colours too, opening up a wider range of
combinations, whether subtle or mad zingy. Flat planes
of colour can look wonderful too when shadows are cast
on them by strong sunlight. Sharp, clean shadows of
nearby structures will add drama and definition while the

dancing shadows of textural leaves from cleverly placed plants add a life and movement to the space.

Concrete block rendered and painted walls are easier and cheaper to build from scratch than brick walls and the smoother flat or slightly textured finish is less fussy. They open up the opportunity to colour up and create a more contemporary garden feel. Sure, paint over ugly existing cheap bricks, but be careful not to commit the sin of covering a lovely old characterful wall. Wooden fences can easily be stained too as it's far easier to reapply than paint because it soaks in and therefore doesn't need preparation (always try a small bit first and

check it doesn't seep through to the neighbour's side!). Garden furniture can also be painted for a revamp and even old stone, wood or terracotta pots can be washed over with a masonry paint to tie them all in together.

Choosing the right colour or complementary combination (two is usually enough) and using them boldly is the key to success. I have experimented with different colours and tones in the UK climate. Our natural light is noticeably different from that of hotter, sunnier climes like the Med, and our winters last nearly half the year. Primary colours may be eye-catching, but our light is rarely powerful enough to set them off properly and can end up making a garden look like a school playground. 'Dirty' or 'ochre' colours warm it up and wine reds and deep yellow ochres can look stunning year-round. Cooler colours, such as light and deep blues and purples, are particularly effective in summer but during the long, grey winter months, will they make your garden feel colder? This is a big consideration if you look out on it all year round.

The lightest of colours in deep shade can completely transform that area, bouncing any available light around and in turn helping to lose the gloomy, dank feel. Even the plants benefit from the added light. I find pure white too strong and demanding and it will quickly look dirty. Off whites with a little natural colour such as shades of taupe, oatmeal or even mushroom tend to work better. If you have a garden with plenty of natural light already then consider using matte black. It may be daring but it's also the most effective of all colours. It recedes well but intensifies any greens it sets off.

Before going the whole hog and slapping it on, just get yourself a few samples of masonry paint and some old bits of board to play around with till you choose the right one. Make sure it dries properly as it will change its hue when dry. Then bite the bullet and go for it. The great thing about using paint is that it's never permanent; if you want a new look or get bored with the colour, you can just stick a different one over the top and completely change the feel of your garden again.

colour wheel

The colour wheel is a very simple tool and especially useful for those who aren't confident with colours but want great combinations (either harmonious or slightly riotous!). Most designers use it as a foolproof way to combine colours, at least to get the basics right within a garden (flower colours, materials and painted elements),

which can, over time, be expanded on and experimented with (e.g. adding in spring bulbs and annual plants as accents). The percentage of plants plays a part too. So, for example, in a triadic scheme (see below), perhaps rather than 33%/33%/33%, go for a scheme of 70% blue flowering and 30% orange flowering (with the green added by all the foliage anyway!). Once you know a few rules, you can throw the rule book out the window.

complementary

Two colours that are on opposite sides of the wheel are complementary. This combination provides a high-contrast and high- impact combination – together they appear brighter and more prominent.

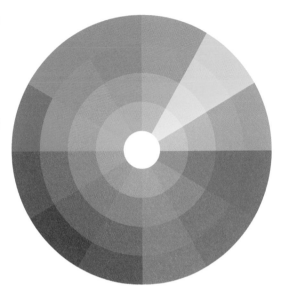

Triadic

Choose three colours evenly spaced on the colour wheel. This makes a high contrast scheme but a little less than with just two complementary colours.

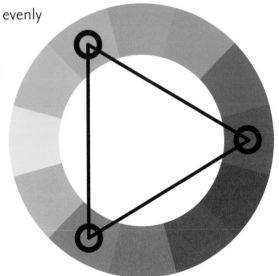

Analogous

Three colours side-by-side on the colour wheel. Safe but can be overwhelming and obvious, so perhaps choose one as a dominant colour and two as accent colours.

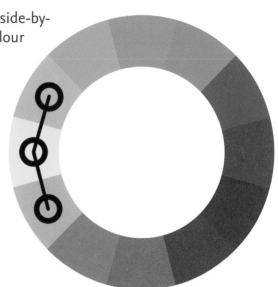

Warm and cool spectrums

This is another consideration but perhaps your garden plant combos can naturally move seasonally from cool colours in spring and early summer to warmer in high summer and then autumnal tones come in later?

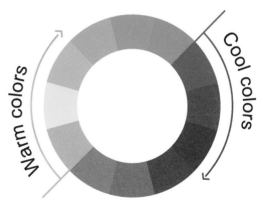

Warm colors

Cool colors

technology

The modern gardener will embrace good technology. Garden gadgets have been slow to develop but there is an increasing amount coming through and we're bound to see more refined products in the future. Sure, they're an investment but they are definitely worth exploring. Some can save a huge amount of time, while others enhance the look and use of the garden and even turn it into a science lab.

Robot mowers

I have recently bought one and am a complete convert. Most mower manufacturers have moved into this sector, improving quality and bringing prices down and I predict an explosion over the next few years. There are models that run off a phone app (so can be worked remotely), map out your garden by GPS and even know what the weather's going to be like! They return to the charger and the more expensive ones can cope with intricate shaped lawns and quite steep slopes. They produce a good quality lawn and use very little electricity over a year and are greener than petrol mowers. They do require installation (smaller ones can be done DIY) by laying a guide wire around the edges.

Solar

The technology and efficiency of solar power have come on tremendously over recent years. LED lighting, and pond and water feature pumps can be powered by solar power; some pumps have a solar panel fitted on the top of the unit while others have a panel that can be placed at a distance, out of sight and where it catches the most rays. Some irrigation pumps and timers can also be powered by the sun.

weather stations

Weather stations have a sensor (or multiple sensors) in the garden and feed information to a base station indoors; ideal for  keen gardeners but also fun. Basic models give indoor and outdoor temperature and humidity, air pressure and moon phases, whereas more advanced models also provide barometric pressure, wind speed and direction, dew point, rainfall, weather forecast, sunrise/sunset times, graphing of weather trends and alarms sent straight to your phone.

cordless electric tools

There is an increasing range of cordless tools (lawnmowers, hedge trimmers,  grass edgers and strimmers, leaf blowers, chainsaws, etc.). I have a couple and find them powerful enough so use them a lot. I find that they are light, very versatile (no power cables to get in the way and quick to set up) and a single charge goes quite a long way. It's well worth buying two batteries so one's charging while the other's being used.

garden cams

Yes, I have a discreet camera that looks out onto my garden! When I'm away from home working, I can still see part of my garden and enjoy what I've planted on the app in HD through my phone or on my tablet.

irrigation

Irrigation systems can be very discreet and set on timers or can use humidity detectors to turn them on and off when it's dry. They have been around for a while but have become more reliable for home use

APPS

There are some surprisingly good apps for identifying plants, whether in your garden, someone else's or just on a walk. Some help you build up a profile of the plants in your garden and what maintenance regime they may require too.

structures

garden studios

Garden studios and offices have become increasingly common as homeowners look to their outdoor space as somewhere to potentially add another room to their property. They're not confined to garden offices or studios either: gyms, TV rooms, libraries, saunas, kids' playrooms, teenagers' dens, you name it – they all seem to be the way to go. It's understandable; they're generally less expensive than a loft conversion or extension and less disruptive, construction-wise. As long as they meet the right restrictions and guidelines, they are usually seen as outbuildings within 'permitted development' so may not require planning permission. I've been asked by clients to design them into a garden from day one, which is always favourable. Some go for what are really glorified sheds while others choose more substantial products installed in a day or two complete with insulation and mains power so they can be used throughout the winter. At the top end are the semi-bespoke and bespoke studios, made to measure with the overall shape, placement of doors, skylights and finishes, etc. precisely as you wish.

I have one so can give you my first-hand experience as both a garden lover and a garden office/studio owner. Mine is boxy, contemporary, cedar clad, light and airy inside with a sliding door, skylight and measures a mere 4 m by 2.5 m. In it, I have a desk, a small sofa, a bookcase and a rack for my gardening tools (which were in the shed it sits in place of).

I thought long and hard about it and planned it well. There are many considerations and details to think about;

most importantly, how it can work with the garden and enhance it rather than dominate it. I've seen many that look as if they've been bunged in the garden, perhaps out of proportion to the space or their style is out of keeping with the rest of the plot. So, here are some things to consider.

Style and design

A studio can be a major garden feature and also creates an opportunity to help define a modern space. The shape and detailing should be slick and simple, perhaps reflecting some of the architecture of the property somehow. Look for clues in dimensions, perhaps heights and/or finishes of existing boundaries to link into. I've seen converted shipping containers used successfully as offices.

If you have a garden studio that doesn't fit with your 'modern space' concept, perhaps there's some simple way of cosmetically updating it. Perhaps keeping the structure but cladding it with a material (timber/sheet metal?) to give it a slick finish, or perhaps it just needs staining a different colour (Scandi black?) or completely covering it in a grid of wires for climbers.

placement and integration into the garden

A common approach is to site a garden studio right across the back of the garden. This can work if you have the depth to plant in front of it to screen and in effect create a false back to the space. In a small garden, however, it can visually foreshorten the garden and, in an informal space, the central placing can have a negative impact on the flow and movement to the existing garden. To help it relate to the garden, consider siting it at 90 degrees, to one side or perhaps two-thirds of the way down the garden, which will create another usable garden area beyond.

planting

Generous planting areas alongside some elevations of
the structure will help soften it and help it to sit in the
garden comfortably, especially when viewed from the
house. It's great to look from inside out through wispy
plants such as tall perennials and grasses too so don't
be scared to plant close up to it or even grow some
well-behaved climbers (trachelospermum, roses, most
clematis) up and over it. The scale of the planting is also
key, so perhaps some small trees or large shrubs taller
than the building itself will help site it into the landscape
nicely and a proportion of evergreens will also ensure it
doesn't become too bare and visible over winter.

Neighbours and privacy

Any garden considerations such as boundaries,
overhanging trees, shade and a garden building near a
boundary should of course be discussed first with any
neighbours that it may affect. The main concerns close
to a boundary or in a small garden are usually its height
and finish, but with garden buildings there's also its use.
Understandably, people are concerned about their own
privacy and quiet, which should be respected at all times.
Something to consider if you're looking to use it to
simply get the teenagers out of the house!

Basic Laws

Outbuildings are considered to be permitted development, not needing planning permission, subject to the following limits and conditions:

- Outbuildings and garages to be single storey with maximum eaves height of 2.5 metres and maximum overall height of 4 metres with a dual pitched roof or 3 metres for any other roof.

- Maximum height of 2.5 metres in the case of a building, enclosure or container within 2 metres of a boundary of the curtilage of the dwelling house.

- No verandas, balconies or raised platforms.

- No more than half of the area of land around the 'original house' would be covered by additions or other buildings.

- In National Parks, the Broads, Areas of Outstanding Natural Beauty and World Heritage Sites, the maximum area to be covered by buildings, enclosures, containers and pools more than 20 metres from the house is limited to 10 square metres.

- Within the curtilage of listed buildings, any outbuilding will require planning permission.

pergolas, arches and walkways

We all love to sit beneath a structure dripping in scented plants; the sense of seclusion and privacy in one's own garden is hard to beat on a balmy summer evening. The word pergola comes from the Latin *pergola*, which means 'projected eave' – a simple way to extend a building to create an outdoor shaded area. Arches and walk-throughs are different to pergolas as they are transitions intended to squeeze one through from one garden space to another. Having said that, if they are long enough and wide enough then why not double up and incorporate a seat below? In design terms these overhead structures form a ceiling to a space, keeping or turning the interest inwards in a small garden or a classic solution to create a more intimate destination in a larger garden.

When you buy your structure, consider what climber you may grow up it before installation. Some structures are more appropriate for some climbers over others. For example, structures with solid roofs aren't suitable for plants that have flowers that dangle downwards, such as wisteria, as they get stuck on top. Over time, the plant can get congested, look uncomfortably squeezed as well as being hard to maintain. Thin wire or plastic-coated structures are fine for tying in roses, but clematis have difficulties getting their tendrils to grab.

Top tips for pergolas and walkways

Style: There are many off-the-peg products in all sortsof finishes and styles (wood, wirework, steel, glass, woven willow). Make sure the structure you buy works with the garden's style, be it contemporary, traditional, rustic, etc. Consider having one

made bespoke or adapted from an off-the-peg product or, if you're handy, make one or customise one yourself (add a colour stain or add some details such as finials). It will add more personality to your garden.

Strength: Some structures are only designed for a few light climbers. For heavier, more substantial long-term climbers such as a wisteria or honeysuckle, the structure will need the integral strength to cope.

Siting: Rather than just placing one in the garden 'cos you want one' consider all the reasons why, which should, in turn, determine its size and placing. Do you want to create shade in a hot spot? Increase privacy from neighbours' overlooking windows? Fit a six- or eight-seater dining table and chairs beneath? Don't be afraid to move plants, re-shape lawns or extend paths and paving areas to make it work and feel integrated into the garden layout. If the budget doesn't stretch to pave beneath, then go for a temporary and cheaper option of using a landscape fabric and some gravel placed on top until you can afford the hard landscape.

Walkways and arches: Don't just plonk one over a path just for the sake of it. They always look best with tall planting, hedging or trellis either side of them so you have no choice but to walk through them, rather than hopping round the short cut! Also, think about what you see as the eye is drawn through them. It may open up an opportunity to place a focal point in the distance but make sure it's tall enough and substantial enough to warrant the attention. Smaller objects (statuary, pots, etc.) can be lifted on a simple plinth to bring them up closer to eye level.

Love the way an arch plays with tone and light, framing the sunny areas beyond!

scented climbers

Climbing roses: If you're planting a climbing rose, then surely it has to be a fragrant one? There are so many to choose from including: 'Climbing Falstaff' (fabulous crimson-purple flowers with a classic old fragrance); for pink, 'New Dawn' is still hard to beat with a sweet fruit fragrance; and 'Madame Alfred Carriere' has white to pale-pink fully double flowers, is repeat flowering and does well in shade too.

Honeysuckle: *Lonicera periclymenum* is my go-to honeysuckle as it's reliable and has creamy-white flowers with purple streaks and, as you would expect, a delicious scent. 'Graham  Thomas' is a simple yellow and white flower, and *L. japonica* 'Halliana' is evergreen but needs a big structure as it's pretty vigorous. Once established, prune regularly after flowering to avoid that knitted bird's nest effect.

Jasmine: The common jasmine, *Jasminum officinale* is a bit unruly and may not be for every structure but if you have room to let it spread and billow then  its strong sweet perfume will instantly de-stress you.

***Trachelospermum jasminoides* (Star Jasmine):** This one's far better behaved. Technically not a jasmine but has small tubular white flowers that pack a similar  powerful scent and glossy evergreen leaves right down to the ground. Needs a little protection from strong winds and cold winters in some areas.

Wisteria: The most majestic of climbing plants, developing woody stems and after a few years in full sun should be dripping in fragrant flowers in late spring. You need to show it who's boss  and prune it twice a year. Many varieties to choose from, including some white-flowering forms.

Sweet peas: Annual choice for growing up a pergola's posts for colour and scent at nose level during the summer.

Holboellia latifolia and *Stauntonia hexaphylla:* A couple of unusual and exotic scented evergreen climbers for protected gardens in mild parts of the country. They both flower a little earlier,  around May, but both have a lovely fragrance followed by unusual fruit after a hot summer.

plants

designing with plants

Plants sprinkle the magic. Their colour, texture, fragrance and seasonality make a garden an ever-changing composition that celebrates life itself. Modern gardens let the garden-maker take control to harness the power of plants to create something personal, unique and very special. It is, however, perceived as the most difficult aspect of garden design. Sure, it takes confidence with plants to put them together boldly but if we break it down into a few basic key elements, it'll help simplify your approach. If you look at top garden designers' planting plans and lists (or images in magazines or on the TV) you'll often be surprised by how simple they can be. The difference between a modern space and the average garden is that the plants are working hard together to achieve a harmonious and balanced goal rather than just being a random collection of your favourite plants all growing together.

style

The site and soil will often dictate the range of plants you can successfully grow (e.g. shady woodland? Or baking hot and dry?), but where there is scope you may want to approach your plant palette with a particular style or mood that you're aiming for, whether it's masses of cool and varied greens to make for a tranquil space or a vibrant colour mix of plants for somewhere far more energised. Once you have the majority of plants in place, there's always the opportunity to play around annually by adding masses of, say, tulips to make a statement for a few weeks. With modern gardens, a timeless and contemporary classic planting style often works best, which I base on the following ingredients.

his planting hierarchy and layering works really nicely here!

Layers

I always work in layers. Trees first, shrubs and tall perennials second and then mid-height perennials down to ground cover. A garden where everything is the same height (often way too low!) rarely has the volume, drama and contrast in light and shade to make for an interesting garden. I don't mean plant trees everywhere, it's a balance between highs and lows and you own your garden to the moon (and beyond) so use it!

Structure

I like strong structure to hold the garden together, around which the more ephemeral plants can come and go. Plant structure comes in many forms. It is often confused with formality, yet many contemporary informal gardens have strong structure too. It may be hedging (evergreen or deciduous) within a garden defining different areas or clipped shrubs that act as part of the green architecture of a garden. It may be a line of tall grasses as a backdrop to a terrace or naturally rounded

shrubs repeated, what looks like rather randomly (but are in fact perfectly placed), throughout a garden to lead the eye. Structure may come in the form of an old characterful tree that's been there for years (see the 'what to keep and what to lose' chapter). There are many ways you could go, there are no set rules, but I always consider the woody structural plants as the backbone of a garden.

Use plants in quantity

As we know, modern spaces often take their inspiration from nature yet distil those ideas into a garden setting. In natural environments (such as a woodland or meadow) a limited palette of plants is often seen repeated 'en masse' as they colonise and freely self-seed around. You'll rarely see a one-off plant standing up shouting 'look at me'! A limited range of plants (perhaps three or five) that look great together repeated all the way through an area can look stunning and if you choose the right blend of, say, grasses and perennials, this will have a surprisingly long season of interest too. Sure, it means buying plants in quantity (which some find impossible to do) but the rewards are there for those who can tame them.

Repetition and rhythm

So, we've talked about planting in quantity, but you also have control over precisely how and where they're planted. Some plants look great in blocks, perhaps holding a corner of a terrace or as a bold statement in borders, whereas many work well drifted or dotted through. Stand back when placing and see if a plant repeated further away keeps the eye moving nicely.

Spacing

The spacing of plants is a question that often comes up. When you buy a plant, it'll have a height and spread but, of course, some grow slowly and some perform differently (growing fast, slower, bigger or smaller) than the label suggests due to conditions. The key is to space the large ticket items and structural plants first (trees, shrubs, hedging, etc.). Individual trees and large shrubs should have space around them to grow into, so try and visualise how they'll mature and what shape they'll achieve. I then infill with perennials and grasses below, looking for a good spread in year two or three. Most perennials are planted between three and seven plants per square metre (which is a good way of working out your quantities). If you plant too closely, you'll be dividing plants soon after they've gone in. The maintenance of a garden is paramount, so of course some plants will need dividing every few years (and it's a way of increasing stock, filling gaps and getting that 'drifty' look) but get the big ones in first and work around them.

Seasonality

Most of my clients ask for 'year-round interest' which usually means 'masses of colour', which is hard to achieve, especially in a small space. Seasonality, however, is a better way of explaining how to celebrate all the seasons through plant choice and I always look at my plant palette to ensure I have a good spread across the seasons and that those with winter interest of fragrance are placed where they'll be seen and sniffed. I only use plants that I know will work really hard and perform for them too, so I try to choose them with multiple seasons of interest (such as deciduous trees with flowers, fruit, autumn colour and interesting bark or long-flowering perennials that also look great in decay).

Specific plant qualities

Across your choice of plants, look for an interesting range of qualities. Plants may have a season when they grab the headlines, but many have secondary or tertiary qualities that are more subtle, so add depth to your planting. Qualities like hips, berries, coloured stems, interesting bark, seed pods, fragrance and autumn colour will all make your garden richer and often more wildlife-friendly too.

Plant directory

There are thousands of plants to choose from for your garden. Which you go for, how you use them and put them together is what will give your garden a contemporary edge. Within a plant species, there are often many cultivars and hybrids with varying qualities (flower colour, height and form, leaf shape, etc.). Here are some of my tried and tested favourites.

Trees for spring blossom

There's nothing quite as uplifting as looking up into a tree's canopy and seeing its fresh spring blossom against a clear blue sky. All flowers are fleeting – one reason we appreciate them so much, of course – but trees in bloom are particularly special; large clouds of colour full of hope for the season ahead. If your garden feels as if it's lacking height, it could probably do with a tree or two.

1 *Amelanchier lamarckii* (**snowy mespilus**): One of the earliest to flower with starry white flowers on bare stems just before the coppery young foliage comes through. It also has a fabulous fiery autumn colour. Mine is multi-stemmed and really earns its keep. Eventual height up to 10 m x 10 m spread, but easily pruned.

2 *Cercis siliquastrum* **(Judas tree):** Clusters of rosy, pink blooms burst from the stems before the leaves come out to create a stunning and intriguing display. From late summer onwards, large bunches of rich purple pods hang from the branches, lasting into the winter. Good yellow and purple autumn colour too. Height 10 m x 9 m spread.

3 *Prunus dulcis* **(almond):** A beautiful alternative to cherry which lights up my spring as it's planted in my street. A small and spreading tree covered in single pink flowers with darker centres and prominent stamen. Excellent yellow and orange autumn colour along with edible almond fruit. Height 8 m x 5 m spread.

4 *Magnolia denudata* **'Yellow River':** There are so many magnolias that thrive in soil on the acidic side. They're not all pink or white either. This one has large creamy yellow goblets eventually (it's slow growing) reaching about 10 m in height. There's a fabulous specimen in RHS Garden Wisley if you're passing.

5 *Cornus kousa var. chinensis:* This is a choice tree with showy white flower-like bracts in late May and then crimson-purple foliage in autumn and strawberry-like fruit once mature. They are slow growing and require a well-drained neutral-to-acid soil. Height 7 m x 5 m.

6 *Prunus mume* **'Beni-Chidori' (flowering Japanese apricot):** One of my all-time favourites and an extremely welcome sight in February. A stunning, yet exquisite small tree ideal for a small garden. It has the most delicate-looking, gorgeous deep pink, almond-scented flowers – a nod to Japan. Height 2.5 m x 2.5 m spread.

7 *Laburnum x watereri* **'Vossii':** This laburnum has huge dangling racemes of bright yellow pea-like flowers in May and June, with each one reaching 60 cm long. It also has a nice sage-coloured trunk and is pliable enough to bend over a pergola or archway and, when it flowers, it looks somewhat like a bright yellow wisteria! Height and spread 8 m x 8 m.

8 *Prunus avium* **'Plena':** A double form of the bird cherry smothered with pure white flowers. It has reddish-purple fruits that the birds love and a fiery red autumn colour. It does get a little large for a small garden but if you have room to let one fully spread and mature, then this one should be high on the list. Height and spread 12 m.

9 *Malus moerlandsii* **'Profusion':** Many crab apples make the perfect tree for a small garden with showy blooms, ornamental (and edible) jelly-making fruit and strong autumn colour. 'Profusion' has masses of deep pinky-purple show-off flowers, reddish fruit and dark foliage that turns a golden orange in autumn, so pretty much everything you would want from a small tree! Height and spread up to 10 m, but can be pruned.

Trees with interesting bark

In the depths of winter, the interesting bark of a tree can hold the interest in a small garden all by itself and may even invite a secret tree-hugging moment or at least a light tickling or a gentle peeling of its papery bark.

1 *Acer davidii* **'Serpentine' (snake bark maple):** There are a few maples called snake barks: *Acer davidii, A. capillipes* and *A. tegmentosum. Acer davidii* 'Serpentine' is a really good choice for the smaller garden, with stunning white-striped purple bark on the younger branches and oval leaves on distinctive red stalks. Flowers yellow in drooping racemes in spring and has a deep red autumn foliage colour. Now that's what we're looking for! Height and spread 5 m.

Nature does it best. celebrate it!

2 *Acer griseum:* A small spreading deciduous tree with papery chestnut-brown bark that peels on an annual basis. Lights up dramatically when caught by the low winter sun. Dark-green trifoliolate leaves turn a very impressive fiery red. Looks great even as a young tree so perhaps a good one for both the tree hugger and light peeler. Height 8–12 m x spread 4–8 m.

3 *Betula albosinensis* **'China Rose' (Chinese red birch):** We all know the ghostly white bark of silver birches but there are many other fabulous birches with a huge range of bark colours and textures. 'China rose' is a beauty with solid pinky-red smooth bark that peels away in clean sheets. Height 9–15 m x spread 4–6 m with a lightly spreading crown.

4 ***Prunus serrula* and *P. maackii* 'Amber Beauty':** Two barks of the cherry. *Prunus serrula* (Tibetan cherry) is the most commonly available and is irresistible to the touch, being shiny and silky. A deep sexy mahogany colour too makes it a top choice. 'Amber beauty' is a larger and more upright tree with a cinnamon and golden yellow bark, white flowers, and red and gold autumn colour.

5 *Cornus mas:* This tree sits right outside my house planted in the pavement and delivers early yellow flowers and deep autumn colour. Its flaking bark is an added bonus that reveals an orange undertone beneath. Height and spread approx. 3.5 m.

Gorgeous, multi-stem form. This cornus flowers before its leaves in early spring. Stunning!

6 *Stewartia pseudocamellia:* A multi-stemmed, deciduous tree with a rounded form. A stunning camouflage-style bark that peels in strips of silver, grey and reddish-brown (a little like a smoother, smaller plane tree trunk). White camellia-like flowers in summer and deep red autumn colour – ticks all the boxes. Needs a sheltered spot in neutral-to-acidic soil. Slow growing but ultimate height 12 m x 8 m.

Trees and shrubs for autumn colour

Autumn should be an exciting time outside the back door, but do you feel that your plot stays mostly green and just fizzles out a bit? A few well-chosen and well-placed hardy and easy to look after deciduous shrubs could help reignite it and once planted will do their job year after year.

1 *Acer palmatum* **'Sango-kaku':** The coral-bark maple. There are many fine Japanese maple varieties with striking foliage colour, with the species *Acer palmatum* high on the list for its unbeatable red autumn leaves. 'Sango-kaku', however, just pips it for me with its soft shades of golden yellow foliage. They look breathtaking against a clear blue sky and this acer has the added interest of pinky-red stems right through the winter. Height 6 m x width 5 m.

2 *Cercis canadensis* **'Forest Pansy':** I'm not a huge fan of purple foliage shrubs as I overdosed on them many years ago gardening in suburbia, but I could live with this one for its excellent variety through the year, climaxing in autumn. After its purple flowers on bare stems in early spring, it has large heart-shaped purple leaves that turn into a stunning showy bouquet of reds, yellows, purples and reds. Ultimate height and spread 8–10 metres.

3 *Hamamelis* **'Arnold Promise':** Not all witch hazels have strong autumn colour so do choose carefully. 'Arnold Promise' has leaves whose colour changes from the outer edges towards the centres. At one point in the process the outer edges are yellow, followed by an intense red in the middle with some mid-green left in the centre. The entire plant ultimately turns a coppery orange. Height and spread approx. 4 m. *H.* 'Diane' is another good choice with deep red foliage.

4 *Cotinus obovatus:* A green, rounded-leafed Cotinus through the summer months, as opposed to the ubiquitous purple foliage varieties. Intense fiery red, orange and purple foliage looking particularly dramatic against its dark stems. Height approx. 6 m x spread 6 m, a nice, rounded shrub if left to grow but can be pruned hard back if so required.

5 *Cornus kousa var. chinensis:* This has everything you want from a specimen shrub. Fabulous white showy flower-like bracts in spring and then purple-crimson autumn colour combined with strawberry-like red fruit. Likes a fertile neutral-to-acidic soil for best leaf tints. Height 7 m x spread 5 m.

6 *Ceratostigma willmottianum* **(Chinese plumbago):**
Squeezed this one in under the heading of 'autumn foliage' but in truth it's an excellent deciduous shrub for general late interest. Ideal for softening the divide between bed and harsh paving. Rounded, yet divided bright mid-blue flowers appear very late in the season and soon after the flowers appear the textural foliage turns a rich red for a double whammy combination. Height 1 m x spread 1.5 m.

7 *Enkianthus perulatus:* *E. campanulatus* is quite a large shrub and probably the most commonly available whereas *E. perulatus* is smaller at around 1.5 metres in both height and spread. Dainty white downward-nodding bell-shaped flowers in spring and then the most extraordinary autumn colours of orange and red as if someone's lit it with a match and stood back. Best on acidic soils.

8 *Vaccinium corymbosum* **(blueberry):** As well as producing delicious 'super fruit', blueberry plants turn a delicious deep crimson in the autumn. Prefer acidic soils but grow in a container and water only with rainwater. Height 1.5 m x spread 1 m.

9 *Amelanchier lamarckii:* This is an excellent small tree/
large shrub with very early spring blossom, followed by
a mid-green foliage that slowly turns to put on a show
of orange and red tints in October. I have a sculptural
multi-stemmed specimen in my garden as wide as it
is tall at around 3 m. Ultimate height and spread of a
standard-shaped tree 8 m x 4 m.

10 *Parrotia persica:* The spreading habit of this large shrub means you'll need some space to let it do its thing but if you have then it's a great choice and worth it for its display of autumn colour alone. The leaves go from bright yellow to orange and then an intense red before dropping and revealing the textural peeling bark beneath. Height 8 m and spread up to 10 m.

shrubs for winter scent

A seasonal highlight for me is the assortment of plants designed by nature to pump out their sweet winter perfume in order to lure in the few pollinators around through the winter.

There aren't masses of winter-scented plants to choose from but if you plan with succession in mind it is possible to have good scent from autumn through to late winter. Some do well in plots too so can be moved around when in flower and then placed in a back-seat position at other times of the year.

Here are ten scented, winter-flowering plants (in rough order of flowering from autumn to winter):

1. *Elaeagnus ebbingei* **(oleaster):** Tough cookie coping well with wind, shade and dry soils once established. Dark glossy evergreen leaves with contrasting silvery undersides that are revealed in a breeze. The autumnal flowers are small but highly fragrant with tones of lemon, ginger and coconut. A friend once said they smelled of Malibu (the drink) and he was right! Height and spread 3–4 metres but can be clipped to size and makes a fine hedge.

2 *Mahonia* x *media* **'Charity' (lily of the valley bush):**
Another tough plant that will grow in any aspect or soil
(except waterlogged). Flowers early from November
onwards and will keep going right through Christmas.
Deeply cut architectural leaves and upright spikes
of bright yellow sweetly fragrant flowers. Eventual
height 5 m x 4 m spread but easily kept to 2 m x 2 m if
pruned hard after flowering.

3 *Sarcococca hookeriana* var. *digyna* **'Purple Stem'**
(sweet box or Christmas box): Sarcococcas are
essential scented winter evergreens flowering from
December to March. The new stems on this one have
a dark purple tinge to them, and the delicate, sweetly
fragrant flowers have an attractive pink base. It forms
a nice stocky plant. Height 1.5 m x spread 2 m but can
be pruned back after flowering.

what a scent!

4 *Viburnum bodnantense* **'Dawn' (AGM) (viburnum):** The bodnant viburnums are fine winter bloomers. This one's sugary, dark pink and its scented flowers are very frost resistant. It may need thinning every now and then to keep it nice and open as it matures. Height 3 m x spread 2 m.

sweet fragrance!

5 *Lonicera purpusii* **'Winter Beauty' (shrubby honeysuckle):** Sweetly fragrant creamy-white flowers appear all over this bushy deciduous plant in mid to late winter. Does well as a wall shrub trained onto a sunny wall. Height 2 m x spread 3 m.

6 *Daphne mezereum* (**Daphne**): A hardy early daphne flowering around February. Violet-pink flowers appear in dense clusters along the bare stems and are followed by shiny red berries in summer. Strong, sweet fragrance. Shady woodland conditions. Height 1.5 m x spread 1.5m .

shrubs for structure

All gardens need evergreen structure to hold them together. Soft, rounded forms are easy on the eye, add rhythm and work well with a host of other plants all year round. 'Rounded' may conjure up formal images of tightly clipped box balls but dome-like forms can look great informally dotted through the garden in varying sizes, heights and textures to keep the eye moving.

Those that require clipping will be higher maintenance (although a very satisfying job), which is a consideration, and you may already have a shrub or two in the garden already that looks a little messy and would respond well to shaping up. Here are some fine choices that are well worth considering if you're adding some in.

Here are five evergreens that respond well to clipping into rounded shapes. Some are fine alternatives to box as the dreaded box blight is an increasing issue for many gardeners.

1 *Ilex crenata* (boxed-leaved holly): Glossy deep-green leaves and there is a new variety called 'Dark Green' with a particularly deep foliage colour. Responds well to clipping and shaping (either once in late summer or in spring and late summer to keep a tighter shape). It's classically used for cloud pruning in Japan, but you can turn it into any shape you want. Full sun or partial shade in any decent garden soil.

2 *Phylleria angustifolia* **(narrow-leaved mock privet):** This is one of my all-time structural favourites for a dark matte green. Small, long, leathery leaves. It's not as hardy as some (grows well where an olive tree would thrive, so does best in milder areas). Makes a great hedge too. Will grow to around 3 m without clipping.

3 *Choisya ternata* **(Mexican orange blossom):** When I first started gardening, this was the most popular shrub around. Glossy, dark-green evergreen leaves and strongly scented white flowers in spring. Grows well in sun and semi-shade. Naturally rounded but clip into shape after flowering, which will often promote a second flush of flowers. Height 2.5 m x 2.5 m.

4 *Pinus mugo* **(dwarf mountain pine):** These can look great, a little like bonsai pines with their rounded forms but the upright candles give them an altogether rougher texture. A few varieties, such as 'Mops' and 'Gnom', will stay quite neat if left (slowly growing to around 1 or 2 metres) but if you want to keep them more compact, clip in spring by snipping off around half the new growth (don't cut into the old wood). Work particularly well in contemporary spaces.

5 **Prunus lusitanica 'Myrtifolia' (narrow-leafed Portuguese laurel):** Better for tight shaping than the standard Portuguese laurel, which has larger leaves. Tough plant that can be clipped into almost any shape: a ball, a dome or more of a lollipop tree with a clear stem. Will reach 15 m in height if left unpruned.

Here are five fine evergreens that grow naturally with a rounded shape:

1 **_Pittosporum tobira_ 'Nanum' (Japanese mock orange):**
I use this plant all the time to hold a corner or to dot through the planting. Try planting a few on a mound to add height to an otherwise flat border and they do well at the base of smaller trees. Great in sun or shade. Carries jasmine-scented flowers in late spring. Prefers a sheltered spot in a town, city or coastal garden and does well on most soils unless waterlogged. Height and spread approximately 90 cm.

2 *Hebe rakaiensis* (**shrubby veronica**): Tough, rounded evergreen that forms a nice tight mound. The small, glossy, fresh, bright green leaves have a subtle yellow edge and yellow margin down the middle that adds depth and texture. Its leaves are pollution- and salt-tolerant so a good choice for a front or coastal garden. Perhaps plant informal pillowy groups/blocks of them if you have the room. Plenty of sun and well-drained soil. Height 1 m x spread 1.2 m. Prune any damaged branches in spring. Hebe pinguifolia 'Sutherlandii' is another good one, similar with sage-green leaves and wider than tall at around 30 cm tall and 1 m wide.

3 *Osmanthus* x *burkwoodii* **(Osmanthus):** Sheer class, ideal for back of border or in a semi-shaded spot. Small, glossy, dark-green toothed leaves and masses of delicious jasmine-scented flowers in April/May. Nicely rounded in itself but you could always give it a light clip after flowering to keep it tight and shapely. Will grow on most soils but prefers a decent fertile soil. Quite slow growing so may be one to invest in if you see a decent-sized specimen. Height and spread 3 m x 3 m.

4 *Viburnum davidii:* This has far larger leaves than my other choices, with a lovely deep veining that makes for a tidy unclipped large dome to around 1.5 m in height and spread. In spring it has flattened clusters of white flowers that are followed by small metallic blue fruit. Tough as old boots and will grow almost anywhere in sun or light shade as long as it's not waterlogged.

5 *Lavandula angustifolia* **'Munstead' (lavender):** Yes, a lavender. They do naturally grow into nicely rounded shrubs even without clipping and are great for low, aromatic hedging. Snip off the flowers as they fade around August, they'll put on a little re-growth before winter and stay shapely and compact. Full sun. This one stays small at around 50 cm high and 60 cm wide but there are many varieties to choose from. Makes a lovely rounded hedge too.

My go-to long-flowering perennials

Herbaceous perennials mainly flower from late spring through to late summer, to add colour and a vibrancy to the garden. They come up each year and then die back into the ground. They are generally clump forming, easy to divide up and dot around. Here are some of my all-time high performing favourites for most average soil conditions.

1 *Verbena bonariensis* **(purple top):** Lavender-purple domed flowers held high, up to about 2 metres, on thin, wiry, almost-square stems that rarely need staking. Each plant takes up such a small amount of planting space in the soil that you can put it in among crowded perennials or between low shrubs and it will force its way through and flower up at eye level.

2 *Anemone* x *hybrida* **'Honorine Jobert':** Anemones are tough, long-flowering and rarely need staking. This one has pure white single flowers with a pink tinge on the underside of the petals. Light-green and yellow centres. Height 1.2 m x spread 60 cm.

3 *Persicaria amplexicaulis* **'Firetail' (red bistort):** Height 1.2 m x 1.2 m. A vigorous plant with slender leaves and spikes of crimson red flowers between July and October. Makes a dense carpet, so ideal for covering ground but adds plenty of height when in flower. Semi-evergreen so may keep its leaves in mild areas.

4 *Eurybia* x *herveyi* **(new name for aster):** An elegant plant smothered with lavender-blue starry flowers with deep yellow centres. Ideal for sun, dappled or partial shade. Height 1 m x spread 50 cm.

5 *Geranium* **'Rozanne':** Large, open, mid-blue disc-shaped flowers with white centres that flowers pretty much continuously from spring through to early autumn. Height 60 cm x spread 75 cm.

6 *Brunnera macrophylla* **'Jack Frost' (Siberian bugloss):** Deep shade? No problem. An excellent choice as the silvery, sugar-dusted heart-shaped leaves will significantly lift a dark space. Light sprays of spring flowers. Height 40 cm x spread 60 cm.

7 *Geum* **'Prinses Juliana':** Geums are ideal for adding a pop into the front of the border. Bright-orange open flowers (great for bees) held on strong wiry stems over the puckered foliage. Very easy to grow and easy to divide and dot around. Height and spread 60 cm.

8 Salvias (ornamental sage/clary sage): Where to start, there's so many! High summer plants sometimes lasting through to first frosts. Nemerosa varieties are short at around 50–60 cm, 'Caradonna' has violet-blue flowers, *S.* x *sylvestris* are generally taller, up to 1 m ('Dear Anja' has mid-blue flowers on dark stems and 'Rose Queen' has pink flowers).

perennial vertical accents

These plants are ideal to introduce long upward (or downward) brushstrokes to a border in a loose and painterly fashion. If you look at a sheet of music, the stems on the notes with their fluctuating heights and spacing will do a similar thing, making it easy for the eye to follow and injecting the all-important flow and rhythm.

1 *Agastache* (**Mexican giant hyssop**): Nectar-rich bee magnet with an interesting minty scent. Available mainly in shades of blue ('Blue Fortune', 'Blackadder'), reddish-pink and violet ('Red Fortune' and new introduction 'Violet Vision'). Long-flowering from July to October. Short-lived perennial and requires good drainage to get through the winter. Heights up to 1 m.

2 *Kniphofia* **(red-hot pokers):** Exotic-looking plants for an upright shot of orange or yellow. 'Bees Lemon' (1 m) flowers from August onwards, 'Alcázar' has slender orange-red flowers (1.2 m) or perhaps the more subtle 'Tawny King' with bronze stems and creamy flowers (1.2 m).

3 *Veronicastrum* **(Culver's root):** Perfect for those slender brushstrokes ending in a pointed tip and structure stays into winter. Require moisture-retentive soil in sun or partial shade, but don't overfeed or they'll get floppy. The tall, lilac-blue *V. virginicum* 'Fascination' (1.8 m) is popular and widely available, while 'Album' (1.6 m) is pure white.

4 **Lupins:** Ah yes, seen lots of lupins at Chelsea the last couple of years. Work well in a more cottage-style garden but versatile too as available in a kaleidoscope of colours, so take your pick. Most reach around 90 cm.

5 *Acanthus* **(bear's breeches):** Tough as old boots vigorous plants for sun or partial shade. Ideal for growing in a block in tricky areas (their large leaves make them difficult to integrate). Easy to propagate from root cuttings. *A. mollis* (1.5 m) has huge leaves and white/purple hooded flower spikes in summer. *A. spinosus* is similar, smaller with more deeply cut leaves.

6 *Digitalis* **(foxgloves):** We all know the common foxglove *Digitalis purpurea*, but there are many other great choices for summer. *Digitalis ferruginea* (1.2 m) has spires of pale orange-brown flowers in mid-summer and large soft leaves. *D. laevigata* has slender spikes of orange-bronze-tinted flowers with a white lip (70 cm). *D. parviflora* 'Milk Chocolate' is later flowering with dense spikes of deep orange to reddish-brown flowers with darker lips (60 cm).

7 *Lysimachia atropurpurea* **'Beaujolais' (loosestrife):** Most Lysimachia don't have the vertical accent we're looking for in this case but this one is an exception to the rule. Long-flowering from May to September, sometimes throwing up slender stems, pink at the base and deeper wine-coloured towards the tip. Likes moisture in the ground. Height 60 cm.

8 *Verbascum* **(mullein):** Short-lived perennials ideal for dotting into sunny gaps and gravel gardens. *V. Petra* has a branching habit covered with plummy maroon-coloured flowers and mid-green flat foliage (1 m). *V. chaixii* 'Album' is reliable and long-flowering, carrying white flowers with deep-purple centres from May to August (90 cm). *V.* 'Violetta' is a little shorter than most so ideal for the smaller garden, 90 cm. Strong purple flowers on spikes that taper to a thin point (80 cm).

perennial umbels

The *Umbelliferae* family has a vast range of plants, but the best known are probably the edibles such as carrots, parsnips, fennel and parsley, to name a few. Anyone who has grown them, let them flower and go to seed knows just how beautiful they can be with their flat or rounded flower heads (known as inflorescence). It's this flower shape that gardeners and designers love for what they add to a border and the introduction of just one or two drifted through in quantity ideally will soften and change the dynamics of a planting scheme.

Here are my top eight umbels:

1. *Ferula communis* (giant fennel): Common fennel and bronze fennel are pretty well known for their fluffy spring foliage and flat yellow flowers. This one's rather special, forming a mound of soft foliage around 1 m tall and its sulphur-yellow early summer flowers can reach up to 4 m in height! Height up to 4 m x spread 1 m.

2 *Chaerophyllum hirsutum* **'Roseum' (hairy chervil):** This is a perennial, a form of chervil with lilac-pink flowers with soft apple-scented foliage. Does best in moisture-retentive soil in sun or dappled shade and will freely seed around. Height 1 m x spread 20 cm.

3 *Cenolophium denudatum* **(Baltic parsley):** Designers love to use this one as it's similar to our common cow parsley but flowers later, from around July to October, and its feathery foliage is semi-evergreen so usually looks good through the winter. Let it seed around where it's happy for a natural look. Height 1 m x spread 75 cm.

4 *Selinum wallichianum* **(milk parsley):** Tiny clusters of pure white star-shaped flowers float above fresh green filigree foliage on purple-tinged stems. A tall plant and less is more with this one, so give it space. Flowers from July to September. Height 1.8 m x spread 60 cm.

5 *Ridolfia segetum* **(false fennel):** This hardy annual grows to a useful height for dotting through borders. Its acid-yellow flowers make a fine foil for just about every other colour you put alongside it and it has a particularly long flowering season from June to September. Sow seed in September for planting out next spring. Height 1 m x spread 40 cm.

6 *Orlaya grandiflora* (**white laceflower**): White umbels with tiny sails at the end of the petals. Great for hoverflies. Makes a great flower too, lasting up to 10 days in a vase. 60 cm tall.

7 *Ammi majus* (**Bishop's flower**): A delicate form of cow parsley perfect for drifting through sunny and partially shaded borders. Hardy annual so sow seeds late summer for the following year. Needs regular watering to get it going. Height 1.2 m x spread 60 cm.

8 *Astrantia* **'Hadspen Blood' (masterwort):** Astrantias are technically umbels yet have tighter, pincushion flowers. They come in a range from whites through pinks into some deep reds and make fabulous long-flowering garden plants for sun or partial shade as long as there's a degree of moisture in the ground. This one has dark stems and foliage that set off the ruby-red flowers to perfection. Height 90 cm x spread 60 cm.

perennial late-summer daisies

Daisies look spot-on in a modern prairie-style border in among ornamental grasses and other sun-loving souls but can also be planted into containers to jazz them up a bit. Rudbeckias, echinaceas and heleniums are my go-to plants in this field, all with the classic daisy flower form with petals radiating from the centre (capitula), but a hybrid of nature's work and human intervention has thrown up multitudes of variations in colour and shapes.

● **Echinaceas**

E. purpurea: A tough species plant. If you have trouble with hybrids, try this one. Fabulous combination of an orange-brown centre and bright pinky-purple petals. Height 1.5 m x spread 45 cm.

***E. purpurea* 'White Swan':** Orange-green centres and drooping greenish-white petals give this a classic daisy appearance. Height 70 cm x spread 45 cm.

***E.* 'Tomato Soup':** Relatively new and said to be a fine introduction, both vigorous and floriferous. Yes, it's tomato coloured, but the flowers start off a little orange and fade to pink. Height 80 cm x spread 60 cm.

• Heleniums

***H.* 'Potter's Wheel':** Deep-crimson petals edged in gold that starts blooming in August and keep going through till the first signs of autumn. Dark-brown rounded central cone. Height 85 cm x spread 40 cm.

***H.* 'Moerheim Beauty':** A reliable classic with large copper-red flowers with downward hanging petals making the dark-brown centres even more prominent. Height 1.25 m x spread 60 cm.

H. 'Biedermeier': Slightly drooping bright orange-red petals with a clear golden yellow edge. The centre is dark brown with a yellow dusting. Height 1.2 m x spread 60 cm.

● **Rudbeckias**

R. maxima: The biggie. Species rudbeckia with waxy grey leaves and a distinctive large pointed central cone. Height 1.3 m x spread 45 cm.

R. fulgida var. deamii: The most prolific flowering Rudbeckia, which, once started, just keeps going and going. Orange-yellow flowers and dark contrasting centres on a stocky plant. Height 60 cm x spread 40 cm.

R. subtomentosa 'Little Henry': A dinky little thing with plenty of flowers with rolled pure-yellow petals. Height 75 cm x spread 50 cm.

climbers

Climbers are essential in most gardens, greening up boundaries and making a garden an immersive experience. Some climbers get a little unruly. Here are my go-to climbers for sun and shade.

● **Sun**

Trachelospermum jasminoides **(star jasmine):** Essential plant! Small, glossy, green leaves from top to toe and small, white, strongly jasmine-scented flowers in summer. Well-behaved too. Height up to 6 m but can be clipped in spring.

Wisteria sinensis: Majestic climber with dangling, scented, lilac-blue fragrant flowers in May. Flowers reach approximately 30 cm long. Also, *W. sinensis* 'Alba' has white flowers. Prune in February and July.

Honeysuckles grow best in full sun like *Lonicera periyclymenum* 'Belgica' with its deliciously scented yellow flowers with a red streak.

● Shade

Hydrangea anomala subsp. petiolaris **(climbing hydrangea):**
Self-clinging heart-shaped leaves turn yellow in autumn
and wonderful white lacy flowers in early summer. Slow
growing – be patient. Height 12 m by a spread that is
easily contained by pruning.

Virginia creepers and Boston ivy: Many to choose from, with some, such as the intense autumn red *Parthenocissus quinquefolia* getting up to 15 m tall by 5 m spread. *P. henryana* is the best for small gardens, reaching 10 m x 5 m spread with lovely white veining on the leaves. Most are self-clinging once they get going.

***Akebia quinata* (chocolate vine):** This semi-evergreen climber, staying evergreen in mild areas and winters has exotic five-lobed leaves and lightly chocolate-scented brownish-purple flowers in very early spring on bare stems. Prune back hard after flowering to keep it to a required size. Ultimate height 8 m x 2 m spread if left.

- **And a climbing clematis for every season!**

Clematis armandii **'Apple Blossom':** Evergreen, vigorous with scented creamy-white flowers with pink-tinged flowers in late winter/early spring. The bold, glossy, dark-green foliage is a huge asset too. Height 5 m.

C. alpina **'Frances Rivis':** A tough yet dainty climber bearing blue and white nodding flowers in April and May followed by silky seed heads in late summer and autumn. Height 3 m.

● Mid-season

C. *montana* 'Pink Perfection': Sweet-scented pink flowers in May/June that show up nicely against the purple flushed foliage. Height 6–9 m.

C. 'Guernsey Cream': Flowering from May to July and often a second flush later with large cream-coloured flowers with a subtle green stripe down the petals. Height 2 m.

● **Late-season**

C. orientalis **'Bill MacKenzie':** A classic cultivar with nodding, yellow flowers each with dark, almost black centres followed by whiskery seed heads. July–Oct. Height of approximately 2 m.

C. viticella **'Etoile Violette':** Masses of deep-purple flowers throughout late summer. Ideal for growing through and taking over from an evergreen or spring-flowering shrub or planted against a bright background. July–Sept. Height of 3–4 m.

● **Winter**

***C. cirrhosa* 'Freckles':** A winter-flowering clematis with small, bell-like creamy flowers with spots of reddish brown. December to February. Scented. Height 2 m.

Roses for fragrance

Scent in the garden has the ability to go deeper and unlock memories of places, people and moments. Just a whiff of some of the powerful old roses often transport me back to my grandmother's garden where we picked roses and sweet peas together. A rose without a scent at all is surely missing half the point of its very existence, a bit like a decaffeinated espresso!

1 **Winchester Cathedral:** An excellent white shrub rose with a hint of pink in the centre. Masses of fully double flowers appear early on this upright bushy shrub and it keeps flowering right through the summer. Full scent is a mix of old rose with some honey and almond thrown in. Height 1.2 m.

2 Roald Dahl: Modern shrub rose introduced last year, which really caught my eye. Orange-red buds open to a soft apricot with a lovely light tea scent. Strong green disease-free foliage. Repeat flowers through the summer. Height 1.2 m x 1 m spread

3 **Roseraie de l'Hay:** This rugosa shrub rose is vigorous and makes an excellent screening plant or even a hedge if you have the room. Dense habit and light-green leaves. The heavy, almond-scented flowers are a rich purple-red with creamy-white stamens. Great hips too. Height approximately 2.5 metres.

4 Fragrant cloud: As its name suggests, it has an exceptional fragrance and is said to be the strongest hybrid tea, so ideal for cutting its large coral-red blooms for bouquets. Height 1.5 m.

5 Gertrude Jekyll: The scent of this upright vigorous English rose is heavenly and often described as the classic old rose fragrance. Strong plant with rich pink blooms. Height 1.2 m or can be grown taller as a climber.

climbers and ramblers

1 **Rosa 'Souvenir du Docteur Jamain':** Vita Sackville-West's favourite, apparently. A deep-crimson climbing rose with upright matte foliage. Excellent on a north wall, repeat flowers and has a fabulous strong classic scent. Height up to 3 metres.

2 **Rosa Albertine:** A fabulous rambler. Strongly fragranced. Fully double, light copper-pink flowers on reddish-green stems in June and July and mid-green leaves. Sweet perfume. Give it plenty of room. Height 6 m.

3 **Rosa 'New Dawn':** A very well-known 'perpetual' flowering modern climbing rose with a terrific fruity scent. Soft pink flowers with deeper pink towards the centre. May be commonly available but there's a good reason for that. Excellent plant. Height approximately 4 m.

ornamental grasses

Ornamental grases can work seamlessly into a range of garden styles. In a rural environment, they will connect the garden to the naturalistic world beyond, whereas in a suburban or town plot they'll loosen and free the planting up, as if a little bit of nature has blown in on the wind. They make the perfect accompaniment to late-flowering perennials and when planted in drifts or dotted through borders will effortlessly link it together, always adding movement with their fine yet voluminous foliage. Grasses are long-lasting plants too, taking the interest deep into the winter months when their skeletal frosted forms sing when backlit by a low sun. Another great thing about grasses is that it's difficult to go wrong; they rarely clash with other plants and never clash alongside themselves.

Here are some of my favourite grass groups. There are too many to mention, but here goes!

Miscanthus varieties: These are stately plants including some of the taller grasses. *M. sinensis* 'Morning Light' has narrow blades with narrow cream edges and reddish-brown flowers followed by seed heads (height 1.8 m), *M. sinensis* 'Malepartus' reaches 2.2 metres in height and has wider arching leaves with a white stripe down the centre (great screening grass). *M. sinensis* 'Kleine Silberspinne' is more compact at 1.2 m with fine leaves and plumes that fade to silver.

Calamagrostis: Upright forms with straw-coloured flower stems. Looks good in blocks or lines for a more contemporary look. *C. brachytricha* has grey-pink tinged plumes above fresh green mounds of foliage. Height 1.2 m. *C.* 'Karl Foerster' reaches 1.8 metres and has almost vertical straw-coloured plumes, whereas *C.* 'Overdam' is a little shorter at 1.5 m and has green and white striped leaves and feathery pinkish flowers.

Stipa: A very varied genus that includes the popular *Stipa gigantea* (golden oats), one of the best tall grasses around. Clumps of grey-green leaves and airy sprays of golden flowers and seed heads in mid-summer, with height up to 2.5 metres. *S. tenuissima* is very different altogether: at 60 cm, it has fluffy silvery plumes that move in the wind (always plant in quantity). *Anemanthele lessoniana* (well, it was and still is sometimes called *Stipa arundinacea* which is why it's in) is my 'most useful plant ever' and the glue to many a planting scheme. It's evergreen, grows in sun or light shade, and freely self-seeds around. Lovely coppery foliage in autumn and winter. Height 1 m. *S. barbata* has amazing wavy silvery flowerheads at 90 degrees to the upright but can be tricky to establish.

Molinia (purple moor grass): Ideal for the wetter garden, although many will do fine on average garden soil. No pruning necessary – I find in late winter, mine just fall over by themselves like 'pick-up sticks'. *M. 'Breeze'* has open, airy panicles and the upright stems light up a fiery orange-yellow in the winter. Height 2 m. *M. 'Transparent'* has the most ephemeral of grasses with a neat mound of foliage and incredible airy, open flower heads. Height 1 m.

Deschampsia (tufted hair grass): Tussock-forming grasses with feathery flower spikes that will grow in a range of conditions including light shade beneath deciduous trees. *D. cespitosa* reaches 1.2 metres and has silvery-purple, fluffy, cloud-like flowerheads whereas *D. cespitosa* 'Goldtau' at 75 cm is shorter and has a more golden flower. 'Schottland' has darker green foliage and upright flowers and reaches 1.2 m.

For dappled shade, look to the shorter *Melica altissima* (Siberian melic) which grows to about 90 cm and then there's my bestie, *Sesleria autumnalis* (60 cm), with its lime-green foliage to lift a shady spot. In deep shade, the Japanese forest grass (*Hakonechloa macra*) looks wonderful planted in drifts as long as there's plenty of moisture in the ground.

General grass care

Never cut back in autumn! Leave the foliage on all winter unless it topples over by itself. Cut back deciduous ones hard in March as new shoots appear from the crown. Wearing gloves, comb through any dead leaves of evergreen plants. Always divide grasses in spring, not autumn, as they can sulk and rot off in a wet winter.

index